Cambridge Primary Path 5

Second Edition

Grammar and Writing Workbook

Garan Holcombe

Contents

Unit	Grammar	Learn to Write	Writing
1 How can we make a difference? page 3	Quantifiers Causative Verbs	Parentheses	Letter
2 How can we make our dreams come true? page 13	Past Tense with *ago* *Might* and *could* for Possibility	Adjectives with Prepositions	Interview
3 How can we deal with natural disasters? page 23	The Present Simple Passive Voice *Too* and *enough*	Quotation Marks	News Story

Unit 1–3 Review page 93

Unit	Grammar	Learn to Write	Writing
4 What makes going to a show so exciting? page 33	Present Simple for Future Events Subject and Object Questions	Conjunctions	Movie Review
5 How can we stay healthy? page 43	Present Perfect Progressive Statements with *wish*	Parallel Structure	Instructional Text
6 Why is language special? page 53	Reported Statements with *said* and *told* Reported Questions with *asked*	Connecting Words	Informational Text

Unit 4–6 Review page 94

Unit	Grammar	Learn to Write	Writing
7 How do machines help us? page 63	Modal Verbs to Describe Future Ability *Could* and *would* for Ideas and Advice	*It's* and *its*	Report
8 How do we know what happened in the past? page 73	The Past Simple Passive Voice Modal Verbs of Deduction: *must*, *might*, and *can't*	Non-defining Relative Clauses	Biography
9 Why does biodiversity matter? page 83	The Second Conditional Embedded Questions	*Although*	Flyer

Unit 7–9 Review page 95

1 How can we make a difference?

Grammar: Quantifiers

SCHOOL NEWS — EVERGLADE ELEMENTARY SCHOOL

THE TALKING LIVES PROJECT—Can *you* help?

I'm sure all of you like talking to your friends and families. Most people enjoy sharing their ideas and stories. But a lot of elderly people don't have anyone to talk to. We want to change this!

That is why Mr. Wilson is organizing the **Talking Lives** project. This is a great opportunity to learn more about people in the community.

Some people have incredible stories to tell, and a few people have stories you'd never believe!

Each week after school on Mondays, Wednesdays, and Fridays, students will visit elderly people in town and spend an hour talking with them about their lives.

If you feel inspired to be a volunteer for the **Talking Lives** project, please speak to Mr. Wilson after school this Thursday.

No student can change their community on their own. However, together we can all make a difference to society.

1 Read the poster. Why is Mr. Wilson organizing the project?

2 Read again. Complete the sentences. Which describes the largest group?

a __Most__ people enjoy sharing their ideas and stories.

b _____ people have incredible stories to tell.

c _____ people have stories you'd never believe!

d _____ student can change their community on their own.

e However, together we can _____ make a difference to society.

Grammar: Quantifiers

We use quantifiers with nouns to talk about the number of people or things.

All students have a talent for something.
Most people enjoy talking with their friends and family.
Some ideas are better than others.
A few students were volunteers for more than one project.
No community can improve unless people help each other.

3 Order the words to make sentences with quantifiers.

a charity / problem / no / solve / can / every

   No charity can solve every problem.

b clean / to / need / communities / drinking / all / have / water

   _____

c happy / others / most / help / to / are / people

   _____

d few / a / houses / water / have / only

   _____

e electricity / some / have / do / not / houses

   _____

4 Replace the underlined phrases with the correct quantifier.

a 4 out of 10 students think they live a very green life.   _Some_

b 2 out of 10 students think they should recycle more at home. _____

c 9 out of 10 students would like to help people in their neighborhood. _____

d 0 out of 10 students have experience with volunteer work. _____

e 10 out of 10 students in our school would like to improve the community. _____

5 Mrs. Jefferson asked students to complete a survey about the Talking Lives project. Look at the results.

The Talking Lives Survey		
	Yes	No
1 Did you enjoy it?	30	0
2 Was it interesting to meet elderly people from the town?	30	0
3 Do you have any ideas on how to improve the project?	3	27
4 Did you make any new friends?	15	15
5 Would you take part in the project again?	27	3

Complete Mrs. Jefferson's email about the survey with the quantifiers in the box.

no   a few   some   most   ~~all~~

Dear parents,

I am very happy to report that 30 students took part in the Talking Lives project last semester. 1 ____All____ students enjoyed the experience, and 2 _____ students said they didn't enjoy it. 3 _____ students have some ideas for how to improve the project, which I hope to hear soon. The great news is that 4 _____ students said they made new friends on the project. 5 _____ students said they would like to take part in the project again, which we hope to do next year.

Best wishes,

Mrs. Jefferson

6 Write about how green your family is. Use quantifiers.

_____ of the people in my family recycle.

_____ of the people in my family turn off lights to save energy.

_____ of the people in my family _____.

_____

_____

Grammar: Causative Verbs

Emily's Daily Blog

Recent Posts | About Me | Archives | Blogro

Don't get me wrong, I like to help people. I really do. But not all the time.

It all started on Saturday morning. I was getting ready to go out to meet my friends when Dad said, "Emily! Come here a minute, please!" He wanted me to help paint the walls of the living room. "OK, Dad," I said. "I'll paint the walls."

After lunch, my little sister said, "Emily, will you cut my hair, please?" "OK, Madison," I said. "I'll cut your hair."

After that, my brother asked me to fix his bike. By then, it was too late to go out, and I was very tired.

At dinner, I told everyone my idea. "Why don't we have our house painted? We can have our hair cut, too. And why don't we have our bikes fixed?" Everyone looked very surprised. "But Emily, you do those things for us!"

1. **Read Emily's blog post and answer the questions.**
   a. What did Emily want to do on Saturday?
   b. How many people in her family did Emily help?

2. **Complete the sentences from the text. Do we know who will do the actions?**
   a. Why don't we _____ our house painted?
   b. We can _____ our hair cut, too.
   c. And why don't we _____ our bikes _____?

Grammar: Causative Verbs

We use a causative verb to say that someone else does something for us. Look at the difference between these two sentences:

I painted my room. ⟶ I painted it myself.

I had my room painted. ⟶ Another person painted it for me.

We use *have* and the past participle of the verb.

3 Write the past participle form of the verbs.

a do   done
b fix   _____
c clean   _____
d cut   _____
e take   _____
f plant   _____

Spelling Rule

Some past participles are regular. We add *-ed* to the base form of the verb:

test ⟶ tested
wash ⟶ washed
mend ⟶ mended

Some past participles are irregular. These verbs do not follow a pattern:

build ⟶ built
make ⟶ made
do ⟶ done

4 Complete the sentences with the verbs from Activity 3.

a We had so many things ___done___ to the house last year.

b My brother has his hair _____ once a month.

c Mom had her computer _____ last week. It's working now.

d My sister has her photo _____ at school every year.

e We had some flowers _____ in our garden over the weekend.

f My jacket is dirty, so I'm going to have it _____.

5 Complete the text with the correct form of the verbs.

> wash   build   paint   repair   cut

What a busy week! On Monday, we had the roof 1 _____, and on Tuesday, we had a new wall 2 _____ around the garden.

On Wednesday, I had my room 3 _____ red, my favorite color!

On Thursday, Mom had the car 4 _____. It looks so clean now! Oh, and yesterday, we all went to the hairstylist to have our hair 5 _____!

6 Complete the sentences. Use causative verbs.

a   bike / fix   My sister ___had her bike fixed___ last week.
b   pizza / deliver   My aunt _____ every Saturday.
c   cake / make   My parents _____ for my birthday last month.
d   house / paint   My grandparents _____ today.

7 What did you have done last month? Write four sentences.

_____
_____
_____
_____

Improve Your Writing

Parentheses

We use parentheses to:
add extra information
> The fundraising event starts at 9 o'clock (but you can come earlier!).

or explain the meaning of something.
> We're collecting money for the WFN (World Fund For Nature).

1 Read the sentences. Which sets of parentheses add extra information, and which explains the meaning of something? Write *add* or *explain*.

a The SFG (School Fundraising Group) meets every Friday. _____

b Please send an email (or a text message) if you're coming to the yard sale. _____

c We need students (and parents, please) to help at the event. _____

d Feel free to bring any items (old or new) to sell at the yard sale. _____

2 Add parentheses to the sentences.

a On a scale of 1 to 10 1 = not helpful and 10 = very helpful, how helpful are you?
   On a scale of 1 to 10 (1 = not helpful and 10 = very helpful), how helpful are you?

b Are you free to help every Saturday or perhaps just one Saturday a month?
   _____

c Conservation charities there are lots of them do very important work.
   _____

d We're fundraising for the NPCA National Parks Conservation Association.
   _____

e We all need to protect parks and trees that includes you.
   _____

Writing: A Letter

1 READ Read the letter. What is the School Volunteer Society doing on April 20?

April 5

Dear students,

Please come to our clean-up day at Greenview Wildlife Park on April 20! Greenview Wildlife Park is home to animals from around the world, including lions, elephants, giraffes, and tigers. But there's a problem—visitors often leave litter behind.

We need your help to clean up the litter in the park to make it safer for the animals and a much nicer place to visit. We all need to take care of the community so that everyone can enjoy it.

Please meet at the entrance to the park at 9:45 a.m. After the cleanup, we are going to have a picnic (if the weather is good enough).

We hope you can all come!

Thank you,

The School Volunteer Society

2 EXPLORE Read the letter again. Answer the questions.
a **Who is the letter to?** Circle the correct part of the letter.
b **Why would you go to this event?** Underline the sentences that persuade you to come.
c **Where is the event? When is it?** Circle the information in the letter.
d **How does the writer say goodbye?** Circle or underline the correct part.

3 PLAN Think of an event like the one in the letter in Activity 1. Make notes.

- What is the activity/event?
- Where is it?
- What will people do there?
- When is it?
- Why should people go?

EVENT

4 WRITE Write a letter about your event to students at your school.

CHECK

Did you ...
- start and end the letter in the right way? ☐
- include practical information about the event? ☐
- include persuasive language? ☐
- include text in parentheses? ☐

Practice Your Exam Skills

Fill in the blanks with the correct answers.

Come help the community!

Have you ever been a **1** ___volunteer___? At Grove Elementary School, we like to help others. Each week, a group of us gets together to **2** _____ our neighborhood. We meet **3** _____ Saturday mornings.

We like to do a lot of different things for our community. Sometimes, we plant trees or help people with their recycling. Twice a month, we pick up **4** _____ in the park (there is always a lot of it).

Another thing we do is raise money for local libraries and schools. We have music concerts and yard sales, but everybody's favorite is Cake Day. **5** _____ takes place on the last Saturday of the month. We make cakes for people to buy and enjoy. We usually raise a lot of money **6** _____ day!

1	A charity	B volunteer	C donation
2	A improve	B improving	C improved
3	A in	B on	C at
4	A disease	B vaccination	C litter
5	A We	B It	C They
6	A that	B those	C these

2 How can we make our dreams come true?

Grammar: Past Tense with *ago*

My Drawings | My Blog Posts | My Favorite Illustrators | **About Me**

LILY'S DRAWING BLOG

Hello! Welcome to my blog! I set it up two days ago. My name is Lily, and I'm 13 years old. I write and illustrate stories for children. I've always wanted to be an illustrator.

I started drawing cartoons ten years ago. I drew in my free time. I even drew at school during my lunch break! "You'll be a professional illustrator one day," my mom used to say.

Two years ago, I invented my own characters—two cats named Arna and Flop. I worked hard on my drawings.

A year ago, my life was pretty much the same as it always had been. I went to school, I played with my friends—just like everyone else. Then, a famous illustrator came to my school to talk to my class! His name was Quentin. I was so excited. I showed him my drawings of Arna and Flop. "These are excellent," he said. "Can I show them to someone?"

One week ago, with Quentin's help, I published my first book. It's called *The Adventures of Arna and Flop*.

My dream has come true. Yours can, too!

1 Read the blog post. Who came to Lily's school?

2 Read the blog post again. Complete the sentences. What did Lily do first?
- a I set it up ___two days___ ago.
- b I started drawing cartoons _____ ago.
- c _____ ago, I invented my own characters.
- d _____ ago, my life was pretty much the same as it always had been.
- e _____ ago, with Quentin's help, I published my first book.

Grammar: Past Tense with *ago*

We use *ago* with a length of time, such as *minutes*, *days*, *weeks*, *months*, or *years*. It tells us how long before the present something happened.

I met my friend Tom a few months ago.

We began learning English four years ago.

3 Complete the conversation with the words in the box.

> ago   a-week   loved   did   a few

Presenter Last week, Lily Murray published her first children's book. She's with us today. Lily, our listeners have some questions. Jon asks: How did it feel to see your book in a bookstore?

Lily Amazing, Jon! I first saw it on the shelf of my local bookstore I **1** _a week_ ago. I was so happy!

Presenter A question from Sophie this time! **2** _____ you have a big party to celebrate your book being published?

Lily Yes, we did! **3** _____ days ago we had one at the bookstore! There are great photos on my Instagram page.

Presenter Oh, speaking of photos, we put one of yours on our website.

Lily Great! Thanks! I took that a week **4** _____. That's my desk at home.

Presenter Clara wants to know this: Have you ever visited the Cartoon Museum in London?

Lily Yes, I have! I first went when I was six. I **5** _____ it!

4 Rewrite the sentences. Use a time phrase and *ago*.

a   We went to the swimming pool the day before yesterday.
    We went to the swimming pool _two days ago_ .

b   My sister left in June. It's July now.
    My sister left _____ .

c   I traveled to Mexico the year before last year.
    I traveled to Mexico _____ .

d   We saw the movie on Friday. It's Tuesday now.
    We saw the movie _____ .

e   It's May now. I scored the winning goal last May. I scored the winning goal
    _____ .

5 **Answer the questions. Use the past tense with *ago*.**

a   When did you last see your friends?
_____

b   When did you last go on vacation?
_____

c   When did you last read a book?
_____

d   When did you last visit your grandparents?
_____

6 **Read about Arthur Weston's life. Complete the sentences using the past tense with *ago*.**

2009—begins playing tennis

2012—wins his first tournament

July 2018—gets injured

January 2019—returns from his injury

Today—July 17, 2019

a   He ____began____ playing tennis ____ten years ago____.
b   He _____ his first tournament _____.
c   He _____ injured _____.
d   He _____ from his injury _____.

7 **Write about important moments in your life (for example, starting school, winning a competition, learning to ride a bike). Use the past tense with *ago*.**

a   _____
b   _____
c   _____
d   _____

Grammar: *might* and *could* for Possibility

"Career," said Mrs. Jones. "Career," she said again, writing the word on the whiteboard. "What does *career* mean?" Everyone put their hands up. Mrs. Jones called on me. I said, "It's the job you do for a long time." Mrs. Jones said, "Exactly! For example, you play the piano, Robert, so you might work as a composer. And you like designing things, Jennifer, so you could be an engineer. We don't know for certain, of course, but these are possibilities."

Sam put his hand up. "Mrs. Jones, how do we know what job to do?"

"What would you like to do, Sam?"

"Um," he said, "I enjoy making things, so I might become … a sculptor!"

"The important thing, everyone," said Mrs. Jones, "is to have an ambition, a dream.

Work hard, everyone, and your dreams come true."

I didn't tell Mrs. Jones about my dream. It's my secret—I'm only telling you, so please don't tell anyone else. I'd like to be a teacher. One day, I might be just like Mrs. Jones.

1. Read Hannah's diary. What do the children talk about in class?

2. Read the story again. Underline *might* and *could*. Do they help talk about the present or the future? What kind of word follows them?

3. Match the people with the jobs mentioned in the text. Are these jobs certain or just possible?

   1 Robert   a engineer
   2 Jennifer   b composer
   3 Sam   c teacher
   4 Hannah   d sculptor

16

Grammar: *might* and *could* for Possibility

We use *might* and *could* in front of a base verb (for example, *go, do, run, see*) to describe future events that are possible but aren't certain. If we are certain, we use *will* instead.

You **could** win the competition.
I **might** visit my cousins this weekend.
She **might** go to a movie.

4 Complete the sentences with the verbs from the box.

> win   go   be   rain   ~~visit~~

a We might ____visit____ my family in New York this summer.

b Marco's team could _____ this match!

c She's very good! She could _____ a professional soccer player!

d We might _____ to Cristina's party on Sunday.

e It might _____ tomorrow.

5 Are the sentences correct or incorrect? Correct the incorrect sentences.

a We could playing football in the park.
   Incorrect. We could play football in the park.

b You could to be an astronaut.
   _____

c I might being a doctor when I grow up.
   _____

d We could go to the movies tomorrow.
   _____

e My mom might change her job soon.
   _____

About Emily

Emily is 11 years old. She lives with her family in Jackson, the capital of Mississippi. Music is her passion. She plays several musical instruments: the drums, the piano, and the guitar. Her favorite instrument is the guitar.

Emily's Dream

Emily has a dream: when she finishes school, she wants to be a professional guitarist. "Music is the only thing I think about," she says. "When I'm not playing it, I listen to it! I'm not in a band at the moment, but I hope to be in one when I'm older. And I'd like to travel around the world. I hope to meet a lot of people! Of course, I don't know that any of this will happen in the future—nothing is certain. But we have to dream!"

Emily's Daily Life

Before and after school, Emily practices the guitar for an hour. On Saturday mornings, she has a two-hour guitar lesson. "I always work very hard," she says. "I'd like to be the best guitarist in the world! Anything is possible if you work hard enough!"

6 Read the text about Emily. Then, write sentences about Emily's future. Use *might* or *could*.

She might/could be

7 Write about what you might do in the future.

This summer, I might

When I'm 16,

Improve Your Writing

Adjectives with Prepositions

After some adjectives, we use prepositions. Examples are *interested in*, *good at*, and *bored with*.

Jack is interested in **sports.**
Lily is good at **drawing.**
Sam often gets bored with **TV shows.**

Note that prepositions are often followed by gerunds (nouns made from the *-ing* form of verbs).

I'm interested in reading.

1 Complete the sentences with *interested in*, *good at*, or *bored with*.

a My sister says tennis is her favorite activity.
   She is very ___interested in___ tennis.

b My cousin gets 95 or higher on every math test.
   He is very _____ math.

c I run five mornings a week with my brother. I love it!
   I never get _____ running.

d My mom reads a lot of books about the history of Ancient Egypt.
   She is very _____ Ancient Egypt.

e My friend Niall has won a lot of chess competitions.
   He is very _____ chess.

2 Look at the table. Write sentences about Clara.

Activity	Good at	Interested in	Bored with
swimming	✓	✗	✓
writing	✓	✓	✗
learning languages	✗	✓	✗
painting	✗	✗	✓

a Clara's good at swimming, but she isn't interested in it. She's bored with swimming.

b _____

c _____

d _____

Writing: An Interview

1 READ Read the interview. What is Noah's big dream?

UP AND RUNNING

Today, our sports reporter Amy Wright is with Noah Thomas. He's a young athlete from Missouri.

Hi, Noah. Thanks for talking to me today. When did you become interested in running?

When I was five years old, I started running with my dad on weekends. We'd only run for 15 minutes. By my sixth birthday, I could run for an hour! I've always liked running long distances; my favorite race is the 1,500 meters.

Do you find running easy or difficult?

I was good at running from the start, but it's harder than people think, especially in hot weather. You have to learn when to run fast and when to run slow.

How often do you train?

Six days a week! I never get bored with it. Every time I train, I know I'm getting better.

Have you won any competitions?

Yes, I have! I've won races in my school and my area. This summer I'm going to run in the National Championships for the first time!

What are your ambitions?

First, to win the National Championships. But my big dream is to win a gold medal in the Olympic Games.

You can do it, Noah! Thanks again for talking to us!

2 EXPLORE Answer the questions.

a How does the interview start? How does the interview end?

b Who is asking the questions? Who is answering the questions?

c Underline the examples of adjectives followed by prepositions in the interview.

3. **PLAN** You are going write an interview with someone you know about. Choose someone who has achieved something amazing. Research the person's life. Complete the chart.

Name, Age, Nationality

Activity the Person Is Good At; Some Things the Person Has Already Done

The Person's Dreams for the Future

4. **WRITE** Write an interview. Include questions and answers. Use your notes from Activity 3 to help you.

Interview with _____

He/She is _____

CHECK

Did you …
- start and end the interview in the right way? ☐
- include questions and answers? ☐
- use adjectives followed by prepositions? ☐

Practice Your Exam Skills

You want to go to the movies with your friend to watch a new movie called *Dream Time*. Write an email to your friend.

In the email:
1. ask your friend to go to the movies with you on Saturday.
2. say which movie you want to watch.
3. say what time the movie starts.

Write 25 words or more.

3 How can we deal with natural disasters?

Grammar: The Present Simple Passive Voice

VOLCANOES OF THE WORLD

Kīlauea: A Very Active Volcano

In 1950, Hawaii became the 50th state of the U.S.A. Every year, millions of tourists visit this group of islands in the Pacific Ocean. They come for the good weather, the beautiful beaches, the clear water, and the surfing.

Those who enjoy vacations here, however, must remember that these islands can be dangerous. Hawaii was formed by volcanic eruptions and has one of the most active volcanoes in the world. Called Kīlauea, this volcano is located on Hawaii Island, which the locals call "the Big Island." Over the last one hundred years, Kīlauea has erupted many times. In fact, it has been erupting continuously since 1983. When there is a big eruption, some people's lives are changed forever. Buildings are destroyed. Roads are covered in hot ash and lava.

The people of Hawaii can't stop Kīlauea from erupting, but they can do their best to stay safe. Special technology is used to understand what is going on beneath the surface of the Earth. With the help of scientists, the people of Hawaii are prepared to leave their homes when the lava starts flowing.

 Read the text. Where is Kīlauea?

 Read and match. Does sentence c tell us who uses special technology?

1. What happens to people's lives?
2. What happens to roads?
3. What happens to buildings?
4. How does special technology help?

a. They are covered in hot ash and lava.
b. They are changed forever.
c. It is used to understand what is happening beneath the surface of the Earth.
d. They are destroyed.

Grammar: The Present Simple Passive Voice

We use the passive voice when we want to focus on what is happening rather than on who or what is doing the action. We form the present simple passive with the present of *to be* and the past participle of the main verb (*made*, *bought*, and so on).

English is spoken around the world.
Millions of text messages are sent every minute.

When we want to use the passive but say who or what is doing the action, we use *by*.

Weather patterns are studied by climate scientists.

3 Circle the correct verb.

WHAT IS DONE TO HELP PEOPLE WHO LIVE IN DISASTER ZONES?

a Special earthquake drills **is organized / (are organized)** in schools.
b Everyone **is taught / are taught** about the danger and how to prepare for it.
c The earthquakes of the past **is studied / are studied** by scientists.
d Buildings **is designed / are designed** to resist earthquakes.
e The sea level **is measured / are measured** to check for tsunamis.

4 Complete the fact sheet. Put the verbs in the present simple passive.

Fascinating Facts About the Earth

- The oceans 1 ___are pulled___ by the moon's gravity, causing the rise and fall of the tides. **(pull)**

- More than 70% of Earth's surface 2 _____ by water. **(cover)**

- Mountains 3 _____ when the continental plates beneath the surface of the Earth move against each other. **(form)**

- Weather patterns often 4 _____ by a major volcanic eruption. **(change)**

- Every year the Earth 5 _____ by thousands of pieces of space rock called meteorites. **(hit)**

5 Rewrite the sentences in the present simple passive.

a People use the Internet all over the world.
   The Internet is used all over the world.

b Scientists study seismographs to make predictions.
   _____

c They speak several languages in Switzerland.
   _____

d Scientists use the Richter scale to measure earthquakes.
   _____

e Phone stores sell many brands of smartphones.
   _____

6 Complete the text with the present simple passive form of the verbs.

sell ~~speak~~ find hold enjoy

Life in Hawaii

Hawaii is a very interesting place. Two official languages 1 __are spoken__: Hawaiian and English. The sport of surfing 2 _____ by many people. Delicious food, like huli huli chicken, 3 _____ on the street. Green sea turtles often 4 _____ swimming around in shallow waters near the beach. There are many festivals in Hawaii. The Lantern Floating Festival 5 _____ each year in May.

7 Write about your country (for example, about its language(s), sports, food, and festivals). Use the present simple passive.

_____
_____
_____
_____

Grammar: *too* and *enough*

The Boy Who Had Too Much Stuff

George could never have enough toys. He always wanted something new.

"But you have enough toys," said his mom and dad.

"Please!" said George. "This one's too nice to leave in the store."

George's parents worked hard. They were too tired to argue. They said, "OK, George, you can have it." When George put his new toy on his desk at home, he said, "You can't have enough toys!"

One day, outside the toy store, there was an old man sitting on the ground. "Why are you here?" asked George. The man said, "Ever since that hurricane in June destroyed my house, I've been living on the street."

When he went inside the store, George couldn't stop thinking about the old man outside. He thought, "I have too much stuff. But that man doesn't have enough stuff." And that was why George organized a yard sale. By the end of it, he had $50.35. He'd sold most of his toys. "I'm happy enough with two or three toys," he said to his surprised parents. "That old man needs this money more than I needed all those things."

1 Read the story. Why does George sell his toys?

2 Answer the questions. Who has less stuff than he needs?

a What could George never have enough of?   He could never have enough ___toys___.

b What did George say about the toy in the store?   It was _____.

c Why did George's parents buy the toy?   They were _____.

d What did George think after he saw the homeless man?   That man _____.

e In the end, why were George's parents surprised?   Because George said he was _____.

Grammar: *too* and *enough*

We use *too* and *enough* to suggest comparative amounts. *Enough* means the amount needed; *not enough* means less than needed; *too* means more than needed.
We use *too* before adjectives:
   I'm **too** tired to play baseball today.
We use *enough* after adjectives:
   My friend is fit enough to be a professional athlete.
We use *enough* and *too much/too many* before nouns:
   There are too many people and not enough sandwiches!
Too many goes with countable nouns, like *chairs* and *people*. *Too much* goes with uncountable nouns, like *money* and *water*.

3 Complete the sentences with *too* and *enough*.

a It's ____too____ hot to stay inside.

b I think this room isn't big _____ for Lucy's party.

c This T-shirt is _____ small for me.

d We have _____ much homework this week.

e We've waited long _____ for Sam. I don't think he's going to come.

f There are _____ many apps to download. How many do we need?

4 Rewrite the sentences with *too* + adjective, *enough* + adjective, or *enough* + noun.

a I'd like to play soccer in the park, but it's wet today.

   It's <u>too wet today to play soccer in the park.</u>

b The movie I wanted to see started at 7 o'clock. It's 7:30.

   I'm _____

c My brother would like to buy a computer. It costs $300. My brother has $300.

   My brother has _____

d My sister is fast. She can win the race.

   My sister _____

e We'd like to have picnic, but it's very cold.

   It's _____

5   **Put the nouns in the correct place in the table.**

money   books   TVs   space   light   things

Too Much	Too Many

6   **Complete the text. Use *too much* and *too many* and the nouns from Activity 5.**

My mom and dad love reading, but I think we have 1 _too many books_ at home. They're everywhere—on tables, chairs, the sofa! "Why don't you buy an e-reader?" I say. "They cost 2 _____ ," they say.

There are only four of us in my family, but our house has thirteen rooms! It's too big! I think we have 3 _____ ! My parents disagree. "We have just enough space," they say. Well, we can agree on one thing: we have 4 _____ (six)!

I like our house. But it's too dark for me. My sister doesn't agree. "No!" she says. "It's not too dark, Leo. There's 5 _____ ! Now close the curtains, please."

There's one more thing: my sister and I have 6 _____ ! We have hundreds of video games, three guitars, five soccer balls … But we don't have enough time to enjoy them all!

7   **Write about what your family has too much, too many, and not enough of.**

We have too much _____

We have too many _____

We don't have enough _____

28

Improve Your Writing

Quotation Marks

Quotation marks are used to show words that are spoken. We put them at the beginning and end of what someone has said.

"Earthquakes under the ocean are often followed by tsunamis," said Miss Smith.

We use a capital letter at the beginning of the first word inside the quotation marks.

Ella said, "What time does the party start?"

We put any final punctuation of the spoken words (exclamation point, question mark, comma, or period) inside the quotation marks.

"What a great movie!" said Jon.

1 Choose the correct sentence. Mark ✓ or ✗.

a 1 Lily said, "Would you like some ice cream?" ☐
  2 "Lily said, Would you like some ice cream?" ☐
  3 Lily said, "would you like some ice cream?" ☐

b 1 Tom said, Yes, please!" ☐
  2 Tom said, "Yes, please! ☐
  3 Tom said, "Yes, please!" ☐

c 1 "Can I have the chocolate one"? asked Tom. ☐
  2 "Can I have the chocolate one?" asked Tom ☐
  3 "Can I have the chocolate one? asked Tom." ☐

2 Rewrite these sentences. Use quotation marks and capital letters.

a Jim said, where are my glasses?

_____

b Dad said, look in your room.

_____

c Mom said, they might be on the table.

_____

d Eva said, Jim, you're *wearing* them!

_____

Writing: News Story

1 **READ** Read the news story. Why did Susan Grey thank the people of Marydale?

THE MARYDALE DAILY NEWS

NEWS | SPORTS | ENTERTAINMENT | TECHNOLOGY | WEATHER

Town Library Destroyed by Hurricane

The Marydale Public Library has been almost completely destroyed by the Category 3 hurricane that hit the town at 9 o'clock yesterday evening. The hurricane went right through the center of town, damaging many buildings, including the movie theater and the sports center. Fortunately, damage to homes was not extensive, although there are reports of some structural damage and flooding of houses on Elm Street and Park Lane. There have been no reports of any injuries.

The Public Library was the building most badly affected. Its roof was destroyed, and the flooding on the first floor means thousands of books have been lost.

The director of the library, Susan Grey, expressed her sadness. "Everyone knows how important our library is: it's the heart of our community. Although we are all shocked by what has happened, we are determined to rebuild this wonderful facility." Susan Grey thanked the people in the community, many of whom were already helping with the clean-up operation. "Together, the people of Marydale can make it as good as new," she said.

2 **EXPLORE** Complete the sentences.

> facts   headline   summarize   interviews

How to Write a News Story

a   The _____ is the title of the news story. It should persuade us to read the story.

b   The first sentence should _____ the content of the news story.

c   The news story should contain _____, things we know to be true.

d   The news story should contain information and quotations from _____ with people.

3 PLAN Research a real natural disaster or invent one to write about. Complete the table with information about the disaster.

What happened:	Where it happened:	When it happened:	What people said:

4 WRITE Write a news story about a natural disaster.

___

CHECK

Did you ...
- use a clear and interesting headline? ☐
- summarize the content of the story in the opening sentence? ☐
- use facts in your news story? ☐
- include information from interviews? ☐
- use quotation marks? ☐

31

Practice Your Exam Skills

Complete the email. Fill in each blank with one word.

FROM: Chloe
TO: Josh

Hi Josh,

Thanks 1 __for__ your text message. It was great to hear from you! I'm so glad you're well. I couldn't sleep last night: I was very worried 2 _____ you! I still can't believe there was a tsunami 3 _____ your city. Places are often affected by natural 4 _____; it's always sad when it happens, but I never think too much about it. But this time, it's your city, and I can't stop thinking about it!

This morning, I saw 5 _____ video report online. The reporter said, "I've seen a lot of damaged buildings; many people have lost their homes. People are shocked by what has happened." I hope the city recovers quickly, Josh.

You know, we never have anything like that here in England. Well, sometimes there are small earthquakes 6 _____ even one or two tornadoes. But they are never powerful 7 _____ to cause this kind of devastation. I'm thinking of you, Josh. Let's Skype this weekend.

Talk to you soon!

Chloe

SEND

4 What makes going to a show so exciting?

Grammar: Present Simple for Future Events

> Hi, Ellie! Are you free this Friday?

> Hi, Robbie! Yes, I am. Why?

> Do you want to go to the movies? There's a movie I want to see.

> Sure! What's the movie?

> It's called *Cape*. My friend saw it last week and said it's awesome. It's about a girl who becomes a superhero!

> That sounds fun! What time does it start?

> It starts at 6 o'clock. It ends at 8 o'clock. We can take a bus to the movie theater. It leaves at 5 o'clock. It gets to the theater at 5:30, so we'll be there in plenty of time.

> How about getting home?

> My mom said she'll pick us up at the end of the movie.

> That's great. OK, then. Let's go!

1. Read the text-message conversation. What is the movie about?

2. Complete the sentences. Do these things happen in the present or the future?

   a The bus _____ at 5 o'clock.
   b The bus _____ to the theater at 5:30.
   c The movie _____ at 6 o'clock.
   d The movie _____ at 8 o'clock.

> **Grammar:** Present Simple for Future Events
>
> We use the present simple to talk about future events that have a timetable (buses, trains, movies).
>
> The play **begins** at 7:30.
> When does the next bus from New York **arrive**?

3 Order the words to make questions.

a is / the / when / festival — When is the festival?
b start / festival / the / what / does / time _____
c trains / when / leave / do / the _____
d time / end / does / festival / what / the _____
e days / how / festival / is / the / many _____

4 Look at the leaflet. Answer the questions from Activity 3.

a The festival is Friday, July 12, through Sunday, July 14.
b _____
c _____
d _____
e _____

Three-Day MUSIC FESTIVAL in the Park!

Friday, July 12, 1 p.m.—Sunday, July 14, 9 p.m.

Special train from the station to the festival at 12 p.m., 2 p.m., and 4 p.m.

TICKETS: $45

5 Complete the email with the verbs in the box in the correct form.

> arrive   leave   ~~leave~~   have   begin   get

The bus **1** ____leaves____ school at 5 p.m. (Please make sure your child is at the school at least 15 minutes before the bus leaves.) We **2** _____ to the arena at 5:30.

We **3** _____ dinner at 6 o'clock.
The game **4** _____ at 7 o'clock.

We don't know exactly when the game will end, but the bus **5** _____ Staples Center at 9:45.

We **6** _____ back at school at 10:15. (Please make sure you are there at this time to pick up your child.)

Please contact me at 675-2244 if you have any questions about the trip.

Yours,

Marcel Blake, Principal

6 You're planning a trip to watch something, for example, a play, a movie, or a soccer game. Write a short message to a friend. Include the following information:

- What day the event is.
- When the event begins.
- When the event ends.
- When the bus/train to the event leaves.
- When the bus/train from the event leaves.
- When the bus/train from the event arrives back.

_____
_____
_____
_____
_____

Grammar: Subject and Object Questions

Questions, Questions, Questions
by Charlie Smith

Do your parents ask you a lot of questions when you come home from school? Mine do! What happened in class today? Who got an A on the math test? What did Ms. Richards teach you in science? When does the school play start?

Mom and Dad ask me so many questions that I sometimes forget what they've asked me and answer the wrong question. Here's an example from yesterday:

Mom: What did you do in drama class today?

Me: I had a cheese sandwich.

Mom: Are you listening to me, Charlie?

I *do* listen, but I'm usually so tired when I come home from school that it's easy not to hear the questions my parents ask me. Besides, I always have homework to think about and my friends to chat with online.

What can you do if your parents ask you too many questions? Easy! Ask them questions: *What happened at work today, Mom? Who did you speak to on the phone today, Dad? ...*

1 Read the text. Charlie gives three reasons for not hearing his parents' questions. What are they?

2 Match the two parts of the questions. Which are subject questions and which are object questions?

1 What happened   a do in drama class today?
2 Who got   b teach you in science?
3 What did Ms. Richards   c in class today?
4 What did you   d an A on the math test?

Grammar: Subject and Object Questions

We use subject questions to find out who or what does something. With subject questions, we don't use the auxiliary verb *do*.

Who went to the concert? — Robin, Hannah, and Will.
What happened after the concert? — The bus broke down!
Who picked them **up**? — Hannah's mom.

We use object questions to find out about what someone or something does. With object questions, we use the auxiliary verb *do*.

Who did they **talk** about in the car? — The singer from the band.
What did Hannah **do** on the way home? — She fell asleep in the car!
What did Robin **say** about the concert? — He said it was the best one he'd seen.

3 Circle the correct word in each question. Is the question a subject or object question?

a (Who) / What won the competition? — subject question
b Who / What did you meet at the party? — _____
c Who / What happened in the soccer game? — _____
d Who / What wrote that book about the time travelers? — _____
e Who / What did you watch on TV? — _____

4 Write subject or object questions.

a Billy spoke to Leah on the phone.
Who did ___Billy speak to on the phone___ ?

b Peter broke his leg.
What did _____ ?

c Lola won the chess match.
What did _____ ?

d Holly saw a show yesterday.
Who _____ ?

e Mia and Mateo painted that picture.
Who _____ ?

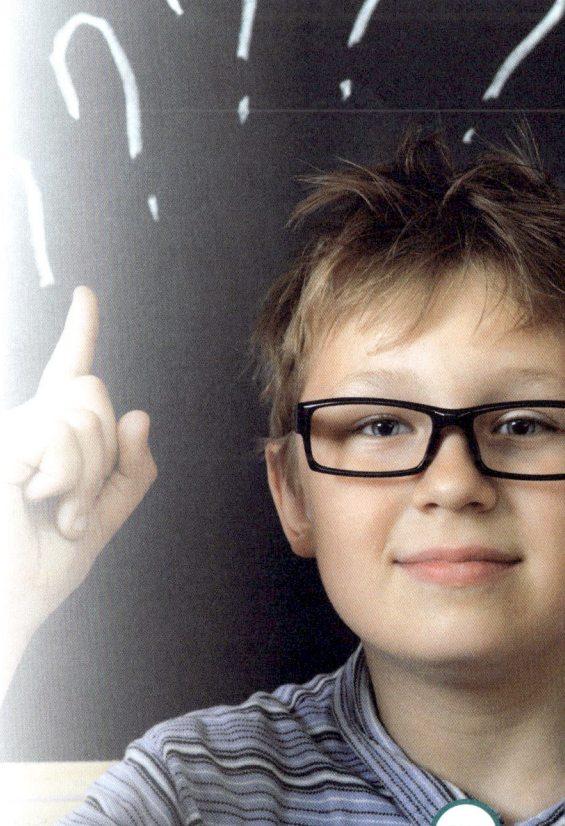

5) Complete the questions with *who* or *what*. Use *did* if necessary.

a _____What_____ happened?

b _____ James meet?

c _____ James say to the famous director?

d _____ called James?

e _____ James think?

6) Read the text. Answer the questions in Activity 5.

My name's James. When I grow up, I'd like to be an actor. A few weeks ago, my acting coach said, "James, the famous Hollywood film director Scott Allan is looking for kids for his new movie. Why don't you go for it?" That's exactly what I did. On Saturday, I flew to Los Angeles with my parents and met the famous director. I said, "It's very nice to meet you, Mr. Allan." Then, I performed for him. He said, "Well done, James. That was great!" A few days later, Mr. Allan's assistant called me. She said, "I'm sorry, but we've chosen someone else to be in the movie." I was sad about that, but thought, "Next time, I'll get the job!" When I got home, I got a call from a film director in London! She wanted me to visit her in London. Two days later, I arrived at Heathrow Airport. What happened? Well, that's another story.

a James went to Hollywood.

b _____

c _____

d _____

e _____

7) Write some questions to ask James about his trip to London. Use the words in the box.

meet   say   happen   visit

a _____

b _____

c _____

d _____

38

Improve Your Writing

Conjunctions

And, *but*, and *so* are conjunctions. We use conjunctions to connect two sentences.
   I like music. She likes art. = I like music, and she likes art.
We use *and* to add information.
   I enjoy going to see movies, and my mom likes going to plays.
We use *but* to contrast information.
   I like plays, but I don't like musicals.
We use *so* to show the consequence of something.
   I'm free on Saturday, so I can go to the concert.

1 Make one sentence from two. Use *and*, *so*, or *but*.

a My sister loves playing the guitar. I love playing the piano.
   My sister loves playing the guitar, and I love playing the piano.

b I like studying math. I don't enjoy taking math tests.
   _____

c I'm tired. I don't want to go to the party tonight.
   _____

d I got an A in science. I got an A in history.
   _____

2 Read Jordan's description. Rewrite the underlined parts of the text using conjunctions.

1 <u>I love swimming. I enjoy running, too.</u> It's good to be in shape! 2 <u>I like playing sports. I do them all the time.</u> Well, let me rephrase that. 3 <u>I play sports six days a week. I don't do them on Sundays</u>—everyone needs a rest. 4 <u>I play football, baseball, and basketball. I don't play golf or tennis.</u> 5 <u>I want to be a professional basketball player. I work hard to improve my game.</u>

1 I love swimming, and I enjoy running, too.

2 _____

3 _____

4 _____

5 _____

Writing: A Movie Review

1 READ Read the review of *Up*. What is Cassia's favorite part of the movie?

moviesforkids.com

Reviews | News | Movie Clips

We review the best children's movies of all time!

Up!
Review by Cassia Martin

Up is an animated movie by Pixar, the studio that made *Toy Story*. It features voice actors Ed Asner and Jordan Nagai and tells the story of Carl Fredrickson, a 70-year-old retired balloon salesman.

After his wife, Ellie, dies, Carl is sad and lonely. When he is told to move out of his house so that new buildings can be put up, he decides to go to Paradise Falls in Venezuela, where he and Ellie had dreamed of going when they were young.

He escapes by attaching thousands of helium balloons to his house, but doesn't know that an eight-year-old named Russell will be coming with him. When Carl and Russell arrive in Venezuela, they meet an old explorer named Charles Muntz, who is not quite as friendly as he seems.

Up is funny and exciting. My favorite part is when Carl ties the balloons to his house and flies away from the city. The movie ends with a big chase. The ending isn't as interesting as the beginning, when we meet Carl, Ellie, and Russell, but I think this is one of the best Pixar movies, and I recommend it to everyone.

2 EXPLORE Match. Then, highlight each part in the review in Activity 1.

1 the title   a who is in the movie
2 the story   b what the writer thinks is good or bad about the movie
3 the actors   c what happens in the movie
4 the writer's opinion d the name of the movie

3 **PLAN** Think of a movie to review. (Choose a movie you have seen recently or one of your favorite movies.) Complete the graphic organizer.

| Summarizing Opinion | Title | Story |

| What I Disliked | What I Liked | Actors |

4 **WRITE** Write your movie review. Use your notes in Activity 3 to help you.

_____
_____
_____
_____
_____
_____
_____

CHECK

Did you …
- describe what the story is about? ☐
- say who is in the movie? ☐
- say what is good or bad about the movie? ☐
- summarize your opinion of the movie? ☐
- use the conjunctions *and*, *but*, and *so*? ☐

41

Practice Your Exam Skills

Choose the correct answer: A, B, or C.

1

Hi Charlotte,
The show starts at 7 o'clock, but I can't come until 7:30. Will I see you there?
Love,
Ana

- A Ana thinks Charlotte can't come to the show.
- B Ana says she will be there for the start of the show.
- C Ana wants to know if she can meet Charlotte at the show.

2

THE WONDER GIRLS

Marta Black's play opens this Friday.

Theater members can meet Marta after the show!

- A Only girls can meet Marta after the play.
- B Only members of the theater can meet Marta.
- C Members of the theater can meet Marta before the play.

3

Young Actors Wanted!

Four or five children (age 10–12) are needed to be extras in a movie.

Email: jonathan@movies.com

- A Children must be the right age to be in the movie.
- B Children of any age can be in the movie.
- C Jonathan needs twelve children for his movie.

4

Why did Beth write this message?

Hi Liam,
We're having a birthday party for my grandpa on Saturday, so I won't be at the game. Sorry!
Beth

- A to invite Liam to the birthday party.
- B to check if Liam is going to the game.
- C to let Liam know she can't come to the game.

5 How can we stay healthy?

Grammar: Present Perfect Progressive

Friday, June 9

It was Dad's idea. At breakfast a few weeks ago, he said, "This family needs to get in shape." Mom agreed, so Dad designed a fitness program for us. He put it up on the fridge the next day. Since then, we've been getting up at 7 o'clock and meeting in the living room, where we've been doing stretches, sit-ups, and push-ups.

Not everyone is happy about it. This morning, my sister said, "We've been exercising too much." My brother said, "I'm hot. We've been doing this for too long." I said, "I've been feeling very tired for the last few weeks." "Come on, everyone," said Dad. "We have only been doing it for three weeks. The beginning is always difficult."

Mom came to the rescue. "George," she said, "I'm tired, too. I think you need to write a new program, one with some rest periods." Dad has been working on the new fitness program since this morning. And while he's been doing it, we've all been relaxing on the sofa!

1 Read Tom's diary entry. What does Tom's mom say his dad should do?

2 Complete the sentences. How long have the actions in a–d and the action in e been happening?

a   _____Since_____ then, we_'ve been getting_ up at 7 o'clock.

b   We _____ this _____ too long.

c   I _____ very tired _____ the last few weeks.

d   We _____ only _____ it _____ three weeks.

e   Dad _____ on the new fitness program _____ this morning.

> **Grammar:** Present Perfect Progressive
>
> We use the present perfect progressive to describe something that we started doing in the past and are still doing now. We use *has/have been* and the *-ing* form of the verb.
>
> I**'ve been playing** basketball for an hour. I'm really tired!
> Mom **hasn't been working** this week. She has the week off.
>
> We often use *for* and *since* with the present perfect progressive.
>
> He**'s been playing** his guitar **for** hours. (Use *for* to state a period of time.)
> She **has been living** in New York **since** 2015. (Use *since* to say when the time started.)

3 Complete the sentences with the verbs in the present perfect progressive form.

> go   make   live   ~~watch~~   read   paint

a I don't like this movie. It feels as if I __'ve been watching__ it forever.

b My brother _____ a chocolate cake all morning. I can't wait to eat it!

c I _____ this book for a week. It's great. I don't want it to end.

d My brother and I _____ to a karate class this year. We love it!

e My sister _____ in Australia since last September. She likes it there.

f We _____ the kitchen since this morning. We only have a little left to do!

4 Make sentences in the present perfect progressive. Use *for* or *since*.

a It / rain / two days

   It's been raining for two days.

b Louise / play tennis / three hours

   _____

c We / live in Istanbul / six months

   _____

d I / learn English / 2012

   _____

e My baby sister / sleep / lunchtime

   _____

44

5) **What have they been doing? Choose the correct words from the second column and complete the sentences.**

a Olivia's tired. She 's been working too hard   .   swim
b My little brother's dirty. He _____ .   ~~work too hard~~
c Jacob's wet. He _____ .   play soccer
d Anna and Alex are cold. They _____ .   do homework
e Harry's bored. He _____ .   build a snowman

6) **Put the underlined sentences into the present perfect progressive.**

1 <u>I exercise, and I enjoy a very healthy lifestyle.</u> Do you know why I am healthy? Well, 2 <u>I eat balanced meals.</u> 3 <u>I don't run to the cupboard every morning to get chocolate cookies.</u> 4 <u>I go to bed at the right time, and I sleep for nine hours</u>—that's just right for me. 5 <u>I swim three times a week, and I run twice a week.</u> I really enjoy exercising; it makes me feel relaxed and happy. Oh, and 6 <u>I do stretches four times a week with my mom.</u> She's an exercise instructor, and she knows exactly what to do.

1 I've been exercising, and I've been enjoying a very healthy lifestyle.
2 _____
3 _____
4 _____
5 _____
6 _____

7) **Write about what you've been doing that's good for your health.**

_____
_____
_____
_____

Grammar: Statements with *wish*

THE BOY WHO WISHED FOR WISHES

Charles Mortimer was a ten-year-old boy who lived in New York with his family. He lived a nice, normal, and healthy life. But he wanted many things to be different from how they were. Every day, he told his family and friends his wishes. He said things like "I wish I was good at drawing" or "I wish I was a fast runner." In fact, Charles liked wishing so much that everyone called him "Mr. Wish".

When Charles was in math class, he said, "I wish I understood math like Laura." When Charles played the guitar at his music lessons, he said, "I wish I could play like Henry." After school, at the pool, he said, "I wish I swam as well as Elizabeth."

One day everything in Charles's life was different. For the first time, he got an A+ in math. At his music lesson, he played the guitar like Henry. After school, in the pool, he swam as well as Elizabeth. Charles couldn't believe it. That evening, on the way home, he turned to his friends and said, "I wish …" "What?" said his friends. Charles laughed. "I wish I had something to wish for!" he said.

1 Read the story. Why do Charles's friends call him "Mr. Wish"?

2 Complete the sentences. Does the verb *wish* describe something true or something that you'd like to be true?

a I wish I _____was_____ a fast runner.

b I wish I _____ science like Laura.

c I wish I _____ play like Henry.

d I wish I _____ as well as Elizabeth.

e I wish I _____ something to wish for!

46

Grammar: Statements with *wish*

We use *wish* to describe things that we want to be different from how they are at the moment. We use the past simple after the word *wish*.

> I **wish** I **was** good at science. (I am not good at science.)
> I **wish** I **could** play the piano. (I can't play the piano.)
> I **wish** it **wasn't** so hot. (It's not the temperature that I would like it to be.)

3 Choose the correct verb. Then, match the people with their wishes.

1. Edward plays music. He has a show later but is missing something he needs for it.
2. Lea loves music. She thinks it would be interesting to learn to play different instruments.
3. Nicky likes all the English teachers but thinks one of them is the best.
4. Bobby likes English but didn't do very well on his last few tests.
5. It rained all day, and Fran would like to go to the park.
6. It's been very hot today—too hot for Jane to go out and play.

a I wish I **was / am** good at English.

b I wish it **is / was** cooler.

c I wish it **isn't / wasn't** so wet.

d I wish I **could / can** find my drumstick.

e I wish I **could / can** play the saxophone.

f I wish we **have / had** Ms. Johnson for English.

4 Complete the sentences with the correct form of the verbs.

a I wish I ____could go____ (can go) into space. I'd love to be an astronaut!

b I wish we _____ (live) in a different city. Ours isn't very interesting.

c I wish I _____ (be) good at basketball. I don't find it an easy sport to play.

d I wish we _____ (have) a dog. They're such friendly animals.

e I wish we _____ (not have) school tomorrow. We have three tests!

f I wish my room _____ (be) bigger.

5 Complete the text with the verbs in the box in the correct form.

> not tell   live   can   ~~be~~   not start   have

I Wish ...

What would I like to change about my life? Hmm. That's a difficult question. I'm happy with things as they are, but I guess there are some things I'd change if I could. I wish I **1** _____was_____ good at sports. All my friends are great at sports, but I'm not. And I wish school **2** _____ so early in the morning. I'm always so sleepy at that time. I'd like it to start later in the day.

Let me see … what else? Oh, yes! I wish that Mom and Dad **3** _____ me to go to bed at 9:30. That's too early! I wish my friends **4** _____ on my street. That would be great! They all live on the other side of town, and I have to take a bus to see them. As for what I'd change about me … well, I wish I **5** _____ black hair (mine is red), and I wish I **6** _____ paint like my friend Richard.

6 Write sentences beginning with *I wish* …

a   I can't play soccer today.   _I wish I could play soccer today._
b   I don't have a dog.   _____
c   I have a lot of homework to do.   _____
d   I'm not good at history.   _____
e   We don't have a garden.   _____
f   I don't live in New York.   _____

7 What would you like to change about your home, school, friends, and you? Write one sentence beginning with *I wish* … on each topic. Use Activity 5 to help you.

Improve Your Writing

Parallel Structure

We use parallel structure to make sentences easier to read. Parallel structure means repeating a grammar pattern in a sentence. For example, we can put all the verbs in the same tense, use only nouns, or use only adjectives.

She likes to read, to write, **and** to draw. (*to* verbs)

She also likes art **and** music. (nouns)

She's happy, friendly, **and** thoughtful. (adjectives)

If we don't repeat a grammar pattern in a sentence, that sentence does not have a parallel structure.

She likes reading, to write, **and** to draw. (*-ing* form, *to* verb, *to* verb)

She also likes to draw **and** music. (*to* verb, noun)

She's happy, friendly, **and** acts thoughtfully. (adjective, adjective, verb + adverb)

1 Rewrite the underlined part of the sentences to give the sentences a parallel structure.

a I like singing, running, and to dance.
   I like singing, running, and dancing.

b My brother spent the weekend climbing mountains, riding his motorcycle, and he played the piano.
   _____

c I like movies, music, and to play soccer.
   _____

d My dad is kind, funny, and he's tall.
   _____

e My mom is a swimmer, a tennis player, and she runs.
   _____

2 Complete the sentences with a suitable parallel structure.

a My sister is tall, friendly, and _____

b I like to cook, to paint, and _____

c My friends enjoy swimming, camping, and _____

d We got to the movie theater, bought our tickets, and _____

e In college, my brother would like to study science, math, or _____

Writing: An Instructional Text

 **READ** Read the instructions. Why are breaks so important when you exercise?

HOW TO START EXERCISING

Do you find it too difficult to start exercising? Do you find it too easy to stop exercising? Then, follow these four instructions!

1 Find a friend. It is easier and more enjoyable to exercise when you do it with someone else. Ask a friend to exercise with you, and then decide what type of exercise you want to do. Friends help each other to keep going.

2 Create a schedule. You and your friend can now choose the best times and days to exercise. Write up a schedule and stick to it!

3 Set goals. Exercise can be more enjoyable and easier to do when we have something we want to achieve. If you and your friend want to exercise by running, swimming, or bicycling, look for races to enter.

4 Take breaks. This is very important, particularly at the beginning. Don't do too much, or you will become very tired and find you want to stop. It is as important to rest as it is to exercise.

OK. That's it! Follow these instructions, and you'll soon be ready to start your exercise program. Exercise is great for both the body and the mind. Why not start doing it today?

 **EXPLORE** Complete the sentences.

> instructions   title   conclusion   introduction

a   An instructional text should have a _____. This is the name of the text.

b   The _____ begins the text. It should include questions to interest the reader in the topic of the text.

c   Numbered _____ make the text easier to read. These should follow a sequence, for example: To make a cup of tea, first fill the kettle, then boil the water in the kettle, then put the tea bag in a cup, and then pour the boiling water in the cup.

d   The _____ ends the text. It should repeat the basic idea of the text, and it often includes a suggestion.

3 PLAN Make notes for an instructional text about training for a race.

Title (Use a *How to …* phrase, for example, *How to Train …*)

Questions to Use in the Introduction (Include at least two.)

Numbered Instructions
(Remember, these show a sequence of actions.)

Ideas for the Conclusion
(Summarize the topic and make a suggestion.)

4 WRITE Write your instructional text. Use your notes in Activity 3 to help you.

CHECK

Did you …
- use a title? ☐
- number your instructions? ☐
- include a parallel structure? ☐
- write an introduction? ☐
- write a conclusion? ☐

51

Practice Your Exam Skills

Look at the three pictures. Write the story shown in the pictures. Write 35 words or more.

6 Why is language special?

Grammar: Reported Statements with *said* and *told*

HOME | ARTICLES | LANGUAGE LESSONS | LINKS

THE LINGUA LANGUAGE SURVEY

We've been visiting schools around the U.S.A. to find out what children think about language learning. We've spoken to over 5,000 children, age 8–11. This is what we learned:

80% of children have daily language classes. Martha (age 10) told us that language learning was something they did every day at her school.

75% of children learn French, Spanish, or German. Daniel (age 9) said that most people he knew were learning a European language.

65% of children think teachers make a big difference. Mo (age 11) said that, although language learning was difficult, his teacher made it fun.

15% of children speak two languages. Alba (age 10) told us that she spoke Spanish at home and English at school.

The Lingua team is excited by the survey results, but we have questions: Should more children be learning Chinese or Arabic? Should all children be bilingual when they leave school? Let us know what you think.

1. Read the text. What does the Lingua team think about the survey?

2. Write the sentences in the text that report the quotations in a–c. In these sentences that report, what happens to the verbs and pronouns from the quotations?

   a "Although language learning is difficult, my teacher makes it fun."

   <u>Mo (age 11) said that, although language learning was difficult, his teacher made it fun.</u>

   b "Language learning is something we do every day at my school."

   c "Most people I know are learning a European language."

53

Grammar: Reported Statements with *said* and *told*

We can use *said* and *told* to report what someone has said. We do not put reported statements in quotation marks; instead, we introduce them with *that*.

We usually change the tense of the verb. We change verbs in present tenses to past tenses.

"I **love** the Science Museum." She said that she **loved** the Science Museum.
"I**'m reading** my new book." He told us that he **was reading** his new book.

We also change pronouns and possessive adjectives.

"**I** want to go to the beach." She said that **she** wanted to go to the beach.
"**I**'m doing **my** homework." He told us that **he** was doing **his** homework.

With *told*, we need an object after the verb.

I don't like the movie. She told **me** that she didn't like the movie.

That can be left out.

He said **that** he liked learning languages or He said he liked learning languages.

3 Circle the correct word to complete the sentences.

a Cathy **said /** (**told**) me that she watched TV with her sister every weekend.

b Ross **said / told** that his dad was from Russia.

c Anya **said / told** the teacher that history was her favorite subject.

d Abi **said / told** her grandparents that she was learning to play the violin.

e Arthur **said / told** that he wanted to go to the park.

4 Complete the sentences with the correct pronouns and possessive adjectives.

a "I'm going to the movies," said Laura.
Laura said that ____she____ was going to the movies.

b "It's my favorite book," said Carly, as she showed it to me.
Carly said that it was _____ favorite book.

c "I like learning English," said Diego, the boy from Colombia.
Diego said that _____ liked learning English.

d "My parents are from Australia," said James, the new boy in our class.
James said that _____ parents were from Australia.

e "I'm having a good time," said my sister.
My sister said that _____ was having a good time.

f "We're winning the match!" said Robin and Delia.
Robin and Delia said that _____ were winning the match.

5) **Report the sentences.**

a "We need some bread and cheese."
Max and Eva said that they needed some bread and cheese .

b "I don't enjoy doing my homework on the weekend."
Ali told his dad _____ .

c "I have to go to the store."
Noah said that _____ .

d "My grandparents live in Italy."
Jenny told us _____ .

e "I'm playing a video game."
Rebecca said that _____ .

6) **Complete the conversation with the words in the box in the present simple form.**

> not want   live   find   ~~enjoy~~   not be

Meg: I really 1 ___enjoy___ learning Chinese!

Dylan: Me, too. Meg. But it 2 _____ easy to learn. I 3 _____ the pronunciation very hard.

Meg: But we're lucky. Na is an awesome teacher!

Dylan: Yes, she is. But I 4 _____ to take the test next week.

Meg: Don't worry, Dylan. I'll help you study. Come over to my house tomorrow. I 5 _____ at 52 Park Street.

7) **Report parts 1–5 of the conversation. Use *said* or *told*.**

1 Meg said that she really enjoyed learning Chinese OR Meg told Dylan that she really enjoyed learning Chinese.

2 _____

3 _____

4 _____

5 _____

Grammar: Reported Questions with *asked*

KELLY'S LANGUAGE BLOG

POSTS | LINKS | GALLERY | ABOUT ME

Friday, September 5

"How was it?" asked Sandra. I'd gone to my first Arabic class, and Sandra wanted to know everything; she loves languages. "OK," I said, smiling. And I told her all about it ...

There were only five of us in the class, and we were nervous. But our teacher was friendly. He was from Tunisia. His name was Karim. First thing, Karim asked, "Do you know any Arabic words?" We told him the few words we knew. Karim said our pronunciation was good! He asked us what our names were. He also asked where we were from. Then, he told us how to say those things in Arabic. He asked us if we had been to Tunisia. None of us had. "Go one day," he said. "It's beautiful." At the end of the class, Karim asked us if we wanted to work hard. "Arabic is a very difficult language to learn," he said. "But it's also a lot of fun." He was right. It wasn't easy, but I'd enjoyed the first class.

1 Read the text. What did Kelly think of the class?

2 Write two direct questions and three reported questions used in the text.

a _____

b _____

c _____

d _____

e _____

Grammar: Reported Questions with *asked*

To report questions, we usually use *asked*:
  "Where are you, Emily?" Yann asked.   Yann asked Emily where she was.
When we report *yes/no* questions, we usually use *if* after *asked*.
  "Do you like sports, Alex?" asked Jo.   Jo asked Alex if he liked sports.
We often change the verb tense and pronouns and possessive adjectives.
  "When is your class, Kirsty?" asked Bill.   Bill asked Kirsty when her class was.
We usually also change the order of the words.
  "Where is my schoolbag?"   She asked where her schoolbag was.
  "What music do you like?"   He asked me what music I liked.
              NOT ~~He asked me what music did I like~~.

3 Write the question the person asked.

  a Nora asked me when my birthday was.
     "When is your birthday?"

  b Gwen asked me if I had any pets.
     _____

  c Dad asked me what I was doing this weekend.
     _____

  d Ellis asked me what I wanted for lunch.
     _____

  e Evan asked me if I liked playing baseball.
     _____

4 Read the reported questions. Which is correct? Rewrite the incorrect ones.

  a Milly asked me what was my favorite movie.
     INCORRECT. Milly asked me what my favorite movie was.

  b Dad asked me what kind of pizza I wanted.
     _____

  c Patrick asked me where was I going.
     _____

  d Kali asked what type of chocolate did I like.
     _____

5 Report the questions.

a "When is the geography test?"
   Mom asked me _____ when the geography test was. _____.

b "Are you going to the movies?"
   My cousin asked me _____.

c "What does Mom want for lunch?"
   Dad asked me _____.

d "Do you know Andreas?"
   The teacher asked me _____.

e "Do you like computer games?"
   Owen asked me _____.

f "Where does Jack live?"
   My sister asked me _____.

6 Write questions to ask Hakim, the captain of the soccer team. Use the words in the box. Then, report the questions.

score   be   be   play

a Which team do you _____ for?   The school soccer team.
b _____ the team good?   Yes, it is!
c Who _____ the most goals?   Cassy, usually; she has 36 goals this season so far!
d What _____ your position?   I play defense

a I asked Hakim _____

b _____

c _____

d _____

Improve Your Writing

Connecting Words

Words like *and*, *but*, and *so* can connect two related ideas in a sentence. *In addition*, *however*, and *therefore* are similar in meaning to *and*, *but*, and *so*, but they connect two sentences.
These connecting words tend to be used in more formal English.

   I speak fluent French. **In addition**, I speak good Italian and German.
   I can speak Spanish. **However**, I don't get much chance to practice it.
   Next year, we are moving to Tokyo. **Therefore**, I will have to learn Japanese.

1 Circle the correct words to complete the advertisement.

English-Language Teacher Wanted

The Westland School of English is a friendly language school offering courses at all levels. Students are welcome to spend as little as a week with us or as long as a year. **1 In addition, / Therefore,** we offer online language courses.

We are looking for a teacher to join our team. You must have at least five years' teaching experience. **2 However, / In addition,** you must have a degree in English. **3 Therefore, / However,** if you have more than ten years' experience but no degree, we might consider your application.

Most of our students are from Europe and Asia. **4 Therefore, / In addition,** fluency in a European or Asian language would be useful.

Please email your application to Antonio Martin by August 1.

2 Complete the sentences with *Therefore*, *However*, or *In addition*.

a We wanted to go away this weekend. ____However____, my mother has to work, so we are staying at home.

b At Mill Lane Academy, you can study several languages. _____, you can spend a week in another country at one of our partner schools.

c I hurt my leg quite badly in last week's game. _____, I can't play in this week's game.

d Although we live in Canada, my parents are from Portugal. _____, I can speak Portuguese.

e My sister can't play any musical instruments. _____, she can sing very well.

Writing: An Informational Text

1 READ Read the text. How did scholars read the hieroglyphics on the Rosetta Stone?

Reading the Rosetta Stone

Museums are places where we can look at important objects from history. One of the most famous objects in the British Museum in London is the Rosetta Stone. What is this stone, and why is it important?

In 1799, French soldiers found a piece of black stone in a small town in Egypt. On the side of the stone was a single text written in three different ways. One was Ancient Greek; another was an ordinary way of writing Ancient Egyptian called *Demotic*. In addition, the text was in hieroglyphics, a style of writing using pictures.

Hieroglyphics can be found on the statues, monuments, and tombs of Ancient Egypt. However, until the Rosetta Stone was discovered, nobody in over a thousand years had been able to read hieroglyphics.

Because scholars knew how to read the Ancient Greek writing on the stone, they were able to figure out how to read the hieroglyphics. Before long, they learned how to read the hieroglyphics on many objects from Ancient Egypt.

In 1801, the stone was sent to the British Museum. It has been there ever since and has been seen by millions of visitors. You could see it, too!

2 EXPLORE Match the different parts of an informational text with the definitions. Then, underline three facts in the text that you find interesting.

1. Key ideas are organized into several of these.
2. This explains the topic to the reader.
3. These are things that are true.
4. This ends the text and speaks directly to the reader.

a. introduction
b. facts
c. conclusion
d. paragraphs

3 PLAN You are going to write an informational text about emojis. Think of ideas for the introduction and conclusion, and research the answers to the two questions. Research at least one more fact of your own to include in your text.

Introduction Paragraph 1 (possible ideas to introduce the topic: what emojis are, how people use emojis)

_____
_____

Facts About Emojis Paragraph 2 Their Invention

When and where were emojis invented _in Japan in 1999_

Who invented them? _a Japanese artist named Shigetaka_

Paragraph 3 Emojis Today

Who chooses new emojis? _____

How many emojis are there? _____

Conclusion Paragraph 4 (possible ideas to end the text: why people like emojis, how to create your own emoji)

_____
_____

4 WRITE Write your text. Use your notes to help you.

All About Emojis

_____
_____
_____
_____

CHECK

Did you …
- write an introduction? ☐
- use paragraphs? ☐
- use connecting words? ☐
- include facts? ☐
- write a conclusion? ☐

Practice Your Exam Skills

Read the text. Choose the correct answer, A, B, or C.

What's the Best Way to Learn a Language?

Marek
When I moved to the U.S.A., my English improved quickly, especially my speaking. Grammar books and language courses are important, but nothing is better than being where people use the language every day. It helps your speaking and your listening! The other thing to do is read. My first English teacher said that reading was the best way to improve your vocabulary. She was right!

Pedro
I'm from the U.S.A., but my parents are from Colombia. I learned Spanish by copying my mom and dad. This means I didn't get bored worrying about the grammar. My advice would be to find a good teacher to teach you the grammar and vocabulary one-on-one. In groups, you don't get much chance to speak, and speaking is the most important thing.

Alina
I enjoy learning languages, and to learn a language, I always do the same thing. I teach myself the grammar and some basic vocabulary, and then I read a few simple books. After that, I sign up to take a language class; make sure you join a big group so you can share the experience with others. When I have some confidence, I go to the country on vacation and start practicing. Start with grammar, I say. Get the grammar right and go from there.

Which person		Marek	Pedro	Alina
1	thinks it's important to learn the grammar first?	A	B	C
2	says that the most important thing is to live where people speak the language?	A	B	C
3	thinks speaking matters more than anything else?	A	B	C
4	suggests that reading is the best way to learn vocabulary?	A	B	C
5	recommends joining a language class with a lot of people in it?	A	B	C
6	doesn't think it's a good idea to be in a big group?	A	B	C

7 How do machines help us?

Grammar: Modal Verbs to Describe Future Ability

More Than One Thing at a Time: Quantum Computing Is the Future

Scientists and engineers are building quantum computers. With these computers, we will be able to solve problems that would otherwise be impossible—problems it would take an ordinary computer billions of years to solve. Marek Gordon, professor of computer science, explains:

Quantum computing is based on quantum physics. It tells us that subatomic particles (pieces of atoms, which everything is made of) can, among other things, be in two places at once!

Ordinary computers use a unit of information called a *bit*; this is expressed as either a zero or a one. However, quantum computers use a unit of information called a *qubit*, which can be expressed as a zero, a one, or both at the same time. This means that quantum computers will be able to work much, much faster than ordinary computers.

One day, these machines will be able to make perfect predictions about the weather. They will be able to help us discover new planets. Unfortunately, they won't be able to stop people from stealing information and may, in fact, make stealing information easier—quantum computers will be able to break our online passwords in under an hour.

1. Read the article. Can quantum computers solve these "impossible" problems now?

2. Complete the sentences. Are they are about the present or the future?

   a With these computers, we ____will be able to solve____ problems that would otherwise be impossible.

   b These machines _____ perfect predictions about the weather.

   c They _____ us discover new planets.

   d They _____ people from stealing information.

   e Quantum computers _____ our online passwords in under an hour.

Grammar: Modal Verbs to Describe Future Ability

We use modal verbs of ability to describe what we can or can't do. To describe ability in the future, we use *will be able to* and *won't be able to*.

   Robots **will be able to** do jobs that people do now.

   Robots **won't be able to** think.

Remember: *won't* is an abbreviation of *will not*, and *will* can be abbreviated as *'ll*.

3 Complete the sentences with *will be able* to or *won't be able to*.

a If we move to Colombia, we ___will be able to___ learn some Spanish!

b Do you think robots _____ think like human beings in the future? I do.

c The class is teaching us so much. After I've completed it, I _____ write my own computer programs!

d I'm sorry, sir, you _____ see the mountains from the hotel room you've reserved.

e I'm worried that I _____ answer a single question on the science test!

f Quantum computers _____ solve problems incredibly fast!

4 Complete the advertisement with *will/won't be able to* and the verbs in parentheses.

DREAMONE—THE SMARTPHONE YOU'VE BEEN WAITING FOR

a You ___will be able to surf___ the Internet **(surf)** faster than ever before.

b You _____ a conversation **(have)** with Marti, your own virtual assistant.

c You _____ while wearing **(swim)** your DreamOne underwater.

d You _____ checking **(stop)** your DreamOne.

e In fact, you _____ your **(put)** DreamOne down.

THE DREAMONE—IT'S ALL YOU'VE EVER DREAMED OF.

5 Write sentences about ability in the future using the prompts.

a People / live on Mars _People will be able to live on Mars._ ✓
b Robots / speak human languages _____ ✓
c Astronauts / travel to Neptune _____ ✗
d People / live forever _____ ✗
e Computers / read minds _____ ✓

6 Complete Kiri's letter with *will/won't be able to* and the verbs in the box.

Dear person of the future,

My name is Kiri. In science class, Miss Arnold asked us to write a letter about what we think human beings will and won't be able to do in the future. We're burying our letters in a steel box. You have found my letter. Read my predictions:

> run   travel   have
> ~~live~~   fly

a We ___will be able to live___ to at least 250 years old.
b We _____. Only the birds will be able to do that.
c We _____ real conversations with robots, which means that robots and humans will become friends.
d We _____ in time; time travel will always be impossible.
e We _____ much faster than cheetahs. Do you know why? We'll have special mechanical legs.

Have any of my predictions come true?

Kiri

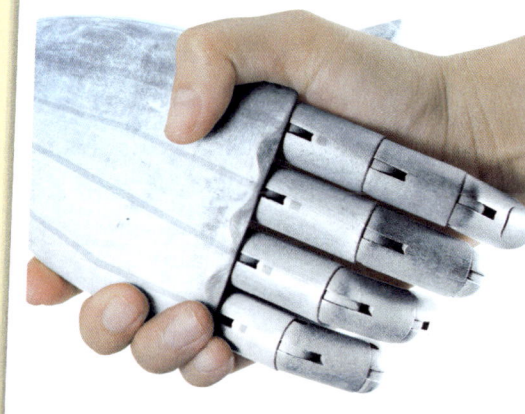

7 Write your predictions for the future. What will we be able to do?

_____
_____
_____

Grammar: *could* and *would* for Ideas and Advice

You Could Build a Rocket

It was Joseph's idea. "Why don't you make a rocket, Ben?"

"But I don't know how to make a rocket," said Ben.

"You could watch a video online," said Joseph.

Joseph and Ben had met in the first year of elementary school. Ben had always wanted to be an astronaut. They were 11 years old now, and although they didn't go to the same school anymore, they met up most weeks. Joseph was full of suggestions and advice. "You could build it in your grandma's garage. You told me she never goes in there. But I wouldn't tell her about it."

Ben worked on the rocket whenever he visited his grandma. One day in early January, he phoned his friend. "It's ready, Joseph!" he whispered. They tried to launch the rocket in the yard while Ben's grandma was taking a short nap, but the rocket failed to launch. "Uh … you could press the other button," said Joseph. That didn't work. "Um, what if you … ?" Joseph had run out of suggestions, and it began to rain. Space remained unexplored, and the cardboard rocket, which Ben had worked so hard to make, got wetter and wetter. Joseph had one more piece of advice. "I would make another rocket, Ben," he said.

 1 Read the story. Where does Ben build the rocket?

2 Find three suggestions using *could* and two pieces of advice using *would* or *wouldn't*.

Grammar: *could* and *would* for Ideas and Advice

We use *You could* to suggest possible solutions to a problem.

> A: I'd like to set up a website, but I don't know how to do it.
>
> B: **You could** watch a video about setting up websites.

To make a stronger suggestion and give advice, we use *I would* or *I wouldn't*.

> A: I didn't do very well on the science test. I'm worried about the exam at the end of the year. I think science is really hard.
>
> B: **I wouldn't** worry about it. **I would** speak to Miss Jenkins and explain the problem.

3 Circle the correct word.

a I **would** / **wouldn't** watch that movie. It's really boring!

b I **would** / **wouldn't** go to bed too late, Adam. We have to get up very early tomorrow.

c I **would** / **wouldn't** study Spanish. More people speak it than speak German.

d I **would** / **wouldn't** get your brother a book, Robbie. You know how much he loves reading.

e I **would** / **wouldn't** put your new guitar there, Hannah. Think of your baby brother!

f I **would** / **wouldn't** buy that laptop. I've heard it's a very good one.

4 Match the problems with the suggestion.

a I'm hungry.   _2_

b I don't know how to do my science homework.   ___

c It's so cold in this room!   ___

d I don't know which subjects to study next year.   ___

e I can't find my schoolbag.   ___

f I want to play tennis, but there aren't any courts around here.   ___

1 You could close the windows. No wonder it's cold—all the windows in the room are open.

2 You could have an apple. But don't eat too much because we're going to have dinner soon.

3 You could ask your sister to help you. You know it's her favorite subject.

4 You could go over to Madison. They have new clay courts in the park.

5 You could talk to the teachers and see what they say about the classes.

6 You could look in the kitchen. I think I saw it there.

5) Complete the sentences with *would*, *wouldn't*, or *could*.

a I __wouldn't__ worry about the history test. History is your best subject!
b I _____ choose this piano. It's a little expensive, but it's a beautiful piano!
c You _____ go to the museum before you watch the game.
d You _____ ask your mom to help you. You told me she's very good at physics.
e I _____ buy that T-shirt. It's too small. Why don't you try on this one?

6) Complete the sentences with *would*, *wouldn't*, or *could* and the verbs in the box.

> explain   start   ask   find   ~~read~~

a I can't sleep.
   You _could read_ a book before you try to go to sleep. That can make you sleepy.

b How can I learn another language?
   I _____ a class to go to and someone to practice speaking with.

c My friend isn't speaking to me since I accidentally dropped his phone and broke it.
   I _____ that it was an accident. Maybe you could help pay for a new one.

d Great! I love the show that's coming on.
   I _____ watching that now. Dad said dinner is almost ready.

e I don't know where the new movie theater is.
   You _____ someone when you get off the train.

7) Read Henry's problem. Offer ideas or advice using *You could* or *I would/wouldn't*.

Hi! Thank you for agreeing to help me. I've struggled with math and science this year, and I didn't get good grades on my exams. I haven't told my parents yet. What can I say to them, and how can I do better in these subjects?

Thanks again!

Henry

Improve Your Writing

It's and its

It's and its are frequently confused. It's is the contracted form of *it is* or *it has*. We use the apostrophe to show that some letters in *is* or *has* are missing.

　　It's five o'clock. = It is five o'clock.

　　It's been very hot this summer. = It has been very hot this summer.

Its is the possessive form of the pronoun *it*. It is not used with an apostrophe.

　　I took the dog for its walk.

1 Read the sentences. Is *it's* short for *it has* or *it is*?

a　It's time to go! ____It is____

b　I think it's nice to live in the countryside, but my friend prefers the city. _____

c　It's been an awesome party. _____

d　Look at this one; it's a beautiful painting. _____

e　It's snowed again! _____

2 Add apostrophes where they are needed.

a　Where is my phone? Where did I … ? Oh, I know! It's in my bag.

b　There was once a monster called Greeb. This monster was yellow, scaly, and huge. Its eyes were like balls of fire.

c　Look at that old castle; its tower is so high!

d　I like science, but its sometimes hard to understand.

e　I like my grandma's cat. Its friendlier than most cats.

3 Complete the email with *it's* or *its*.

Hi Ellie,

Are you still coming with us to see the movie tonight? **1** ____It's____ playing at the new Vista Cinema at 7 o'clock. Do you know that theater? **2** _____ next to the museum at the bottom of the hill. You can't miss it. We'll be in the diner next to the theater at 6 o'clock. **3** _____ a great place; **4** _____ walls are bright orange!

By the way, did you leave your book at my house yesterday? I found a book on the kitchen table. **5** _____ called *The Zone*. **6** _____ cover is black and red. Let me know, and I'll bring it tonight.

See you later!

Georgia

Writing: A Report

1 READ Read the report. What is the difference between a simple machine and a complex machine?

Name: Mason Reynolds
Report Topic: The Machines Exhibition at the Science Museum

Last Monday, my class went to the Science Museum in Fairview to see the exhibition on machines. It was a fascinating trip.

The exhibition is about the different types of machines that we use every day. We learned about simple machines, like levers and pulleys. These are the basic devices that help us move or lift things. We also learned about complex machines, like a pair of scissors or a bicycle. Complex machines are made up of two or more simple machines.

My favorite part of the exhibition was the display of clocks. The oldest one was made in the 1700s. It's called a longcase clock. Our guide explained that the clock runs for eight days before you need to wind it up again.

We don't need such big clocks, but they are more beautiful than the ones on our phones. I would love to have a longcase clock in my bedroom!

2 EXPLORE Answer the questions.

a   Where did Mason go and when?

b   What was his overall comment about the trip?

c   What did Mason say the exhibition was about?

d   What was Mason's favorite object in the exhibition, and how did he describe it?

e   What is Mason's opinion of his favorite object from the exhibition?

3. **PLAN** Imagine you recently went to an exhibition with your school. You learned about a complex machine that people use every day: the bicycle. You saw these three bikes. Use the pictures and your own ideas to make notes that you can use when writing your report.

- Location and Date of the Trip
- Description of the Exhibition
- Favorite Part of the Exhibition
- Opinion on Favorite Part of the Exhibition
- Overall Comment About the Exhibition

The penny-farthing (one of the first bicycles, made in the 1860s and 1870s)

The safety bike (invented in the 1880s, modern bikes are based on this design)

Racing bike (the type that cyclists use in competitions)

4. **WRITE** Write your report.

CHECK

Did you …
- include your name and the topic of the report?
- include a date and a location for the trip you wrote about?
- describe the exhibition you saw?
- describe your favorite part of the exhibition?
- give your opinion of your favorite part?
- use *it's* and *its* correctly?

Practice Your Exam Skills

Read the text. Choose the correct answer.

Naomi Page designs robots for the health-care and car industries. Our technology reporter, Brandon Cooper, went to meet her.

How did you get into robotics?

Math and science were my favorite subjects and the ones I was the best at. I went to college to study engineering and thought I would end up building bridges. But in my last year of college, I took a robotics class. From the first day, I knew it was for me.

Do you enjoy your job?

I love it! It isn't easy, but it's important and exciting. We are helping to make the future. Nothing will be the same as it was, and I'm right at the center of the change.

What jobs will robots be able to do in the future?

I think they will be able to drive cars and buses. Trains, too. I also think they'll be able to go to classrooms and teach children. And I think they'll take care of people in hospitals.

What advice do you have for someone who wants to work in your industry?

Before you apply to college, you could find a robotics company and volunteer to spend a week there helping out. That will give you some idea of whether the work is right for you.

1 What does Naomi say about college?

A She went there to study math.
B She studied robotics during her first year.
C She liked the robotics class immediately.

2 Naomi says her job is

A easy for her to do.
B exciting because things are changing.
C not important at the present time.

3 What does Naomi say about robots in the future?

A They will work in schools.
B People will take care of them.
C Robots won't be able to drive trains.

4 Naomi says that, if you want to work in robotics, you could

A volunteer at a robotics company to see if you like the work.
B contact a robotics company after you apply to college.
C try to get a job at a robotics company before you go to college.

8 How do we know what happened in the past?

Grammar: The Past Simple Passive

The Jewel Thief

CHAPTER ONE: An Unexpected Arrival

Hidden in the tomb, a mile beneath the surface of the Earth, we found it—the gold jewelry buried with the Forgotten Pharaoh of Ancient Egypt. "Aunt Gertrude!" shouted Anya. "Come quick! Quick!" I ran my fingers across the statue; it was cold to the touch. It had been there for thousands of years!

We didn't notice Aunt Gertrude come in. "You found it!" she said. "You found … !" The light from her flashlight lit up her eyes; she looked excited.

"The tomb was built around 3000 BCE. Tombs like this were made for the pharaohs. The pharaohs were buried with gold jewelry, clothes, even food," she said. "And it was discovered on August 3, 2018, by Aunt Gertrude, Anya, and Hector!" I said. "And it was taken by me!" said a voice in the dark. We turned around. Standing in front of us, a flashlight in his hand, was our aunt's boss, the director of the Museum of Artifacts. "Conrad!" said Aunt Gertrude. "What on earth are you doing here?"

1 Read the opening chapter of the novel. Who is Conrad?

2 Answer the questions using full sentences. Do the answers say who did the actions?

a When was the tomb built? _____

b Who were tombs like this made for? _____

c What were the pharaohs buried with? _____

> **Grammar:** The Past Simple Passive
>
> We use the past simple passive when we want to focus on what happened rather than on who or what was responsible for the action (often because this who or what is unknown or unimportant). We form the past simple passive with the past of *to be* and the past participle of the verb.
>
> **The Colosseum in Rome was built** around two thousand years ago.
> **The first text message was sent** in 1992.
>
> When we want to use the passive but also want to say who or what is responsible for the action, we use *by*.
>
> **The detective Sherlock Holmes was created by** the Scottish writer Arthur Conan Doyle.

3 Complete these sentences with the correct form of *to be*.

a Our house ___was___ built in the late 19th century.
b The buildings on our street _____ built at different times.
c The newest buildings _____ constructed five years ago.
d Five years ago, a tree in our yard _____ blown down in a big storm.
e Our new kitchen _____ designed by my aunt.

4 Complete the text with the verbs in the past simple passive form.

Machu Picchu is located in the Andes Mountains in Peru. These ruins of an Incan town 1 ___were___ never ___discovered___ (discover) by the conquistadors, the Spanish explorers who went to the Americas in the 16th and 17th centuries.

The buildings of Machu Picchu 2 _____ probably _____ (build) in the 15th century. Then, at some point, people left the town. Nobody knows why the town 3 _____ (abandon). In 1915, an American academic, Hiram Bingham, found the site. He 4 _____ (help) by a local man named Melchor Arteaga.

In 1983, Machu Picchu 5 _____ (name) a World Heritage Site by the United Nations Educational, Scientific and Cultural Organization.

5 Complete the text. Use the verbs in the box in the past simple passive form.

give ~~design~~ make play use

The Les Paul guitar **1** _was designed_ in the early 1950s. Originally, the tops were gold. Later, other colors **2** _____. In the 1960s, these guitars became very popular and **3** _____ by famous guitarists. My Les Paul **4** _____ in 2013. I **5** _____ it for my birthday.

6 Use the past simple passive to rewrite the sentences. Use *by* when there is a specific person.

a People built the castle in our town in the 13th century.
_____

b Tim Berners-Lee invented the World Wide Web in 1989.
_____

c Someone stole my dad's smartphone and laptop last week.
_____

d They canceled all the trains yesterday because of the snow.
_____

e Shakespeare wrote *Antony and Cleopatra* in 1607.
_____

7 Use the information in the fact file to write about Pompeii. Use the past simple, including the past simple passive.

Pompeii was settled in the 6th century BCE.
_____
_____
_____
_____
_____

POMPEII FACT FILE

6th century BCE	People settle Pompeii.
79 CE	Mount Vesuvius erupts. Lava buries buildings and people.
1748	Excavation of the site starts. People find very few bodies.
1980s	People do further excavations. They find hundreds of bodies.
1997	UNESCO names Pompeii a World Heritage Site.

Grammar: Modal Verbs of Deduction: *must*, *might*, and *can't*

Wednesday, April 22nd

In history today, Miss Demir brought in a silver coin. "This coin's been in my family for many years," she said. "It gave me my interest in history." We passed the coin around.

"This can't be real!" said Harry, who never believes anything. "A real coin would be in a museum."

"Do you think it's impossible that the coin is real?" said Miss Demir.

"Uh … ," said Harry. "It might be real. It looks real."

"This might be a coin from Ancient Greece," said Maja, who isn't always sure about things .

"Why do you think that?" said Miss Demir. "Is there any evidence?"

"It looks similar to an old Greek coin."

"Actually, it's not that old, Maja."

"It must be a coin from the Ottoman Empire," said Lena, confidently.

"Why do you think that?" asked Miss Demir.

"The writing on the coin looks like Arabic. And you're from Türkiye, Miss Demir, and Türkiye was created at the end of the Ottoman Empire."

"Good thinking! You're right," said Miss Demir. "This is an Ottoman coin, from the early 19th century."

1 Read Luke's diary entry. Which century is the coin from?

2 Match the sentence with the speaker. Which speaker is least certain?
- a "This might be a coin from Ancient Greece."
- b "It must be a coin from the Ottoman Empire."
- c "This can't be real!"

1 Harry
2 Maja
3 Lena

76

Grammar: Modal Verbs of Deduction: *must*, *might*, and *can't*

We use modal verbs of deduction when we're making guesses based on facts.
We use *must* when the existence of strong evidence makes us sure that something is true.
   There's no answer at the door. She must be out.
We use *might* when we think something is possible but we are not sure.
   Have you looked in the kitchen? Your coat might be in there.
We use *can't* when we are sure that something is not possible.
   This can't be a helmet from the Bronze Age. It doesn't look old enough.

3 Complete the sentences with *must* or *can't*.

a They've been playing in the sun all afternoon. They ___must___ be tired.

b I _____ have the wrong code for the door. I've tried the number four times, and the door still won't open.

c You _____ be thirsty anymore, Daniel. You just drank two glasses of water!

d Jack _____ be very happy at the moment; his team lost the big soccer game this weekend.

e This _____ be where we'll find the Picasso paintings. Look! The sign says "20th Century Art."

f It _____ be great to live right next to the ocean; you can go swimming every day!

4 Circle the correct word.

a Dad says the painting we found in the attic **can't / must / (might)** be by Picasso because it looks like his other paintings.

b It looks like Andrea, but it **can't / must / might** be her. She's in Canada!

c I wonder why Sara wasn't in school today. She **can't / must / might** be sick. Or maybe she hasn't come back from her trip yet.

d Oh, no! It's his birthday, and he doesn't feel well. He **can't / must / might** be really unhappy.

e It **can't / must / might** be Dad calling me because he said he'd call later than this.

f Arthur **can't / must / might** be very happy. He got an A on all his exams!

5) **Read and complete the sentences using *must*, *might*, and *can't* with *be*.**

Ben failed three important exams, won a big tennis tournament, and read a book about the U.S.A.

a __He can't be__ happy about his exam grades.

b _____ pleased about the tennis tournament.

c _____ going on vacation to the U.S.A.

Laura won a speaking competition, lost her phone, and talked to her friends about her mom's birthday.

d _____ very happy about the speaking competition.

e _____ pleased about her new smartphone.

f _____ organizing a surprise birthday party for her mom.

6) **Complete the sentences with *must*, *might*, or *can't*.**

a Perhaps Olga is from Poland. I know a few people from Poland with that name.
Olga __might be from Poland.__

b It's not possible that Leo is hungry. He's just had a big sandwich for lunch.
Leo _____

c Perhaps the video game is in the living room. I've looked everywhere else but can't find it. The video game _____

d I'm sure Carrie has a new dog. I've seen her in the park with it a few times.
Carrie _____

7) **Make three deductions about Sara in your notebook. Use *must be*, *might be*, or *can't be* and the words in the box. Give one or more reasons for each deduction.**

> out of the house   swimming pool   phone on silent   the movie theater

Sara used to go swimming on Fridays, but the pool has been closed. She's been going to the movies instead. When she does, she always switches off her phone. It's Friday, and Sara isn't answering. You rang her doorbell, but no one's there.

Improve Your Writing

Non-defining Relative Clauses

We use non-defining relative clauses to add extra information to a sentence. In non-defining relative clauses, we use the relative pronouns *who* and *which*. *Who* is for people. *Which* is for things and places. Commas indicate that the information is not essential.

  In the summer, we visited Grand Canyon National Park, which I loved.
  My cousin, who lives in Seattle, is two years older than me.
  I went to a Renaissance exhibition, which my teacher told me about.

We do not use *that* with a non-defining relative clause.

1 Circle *who* or *which*.

a   Heinrich Schliemann, **(who)** / **which** discovered the site of Troy, helped develop archeology in the 19th century.

b   My father was born in Wales, **who** / **which** is one of the four parts of the U.K.

c   My cousin Greta, **who** / **which** is a historian, moved to Bologna, in Italy.

d   Mexico, **who** / **which** is one of three countries in North America, is where my cousins live.

e   My grandmother, **who** / **which** lives next door to us, knows a lot about Africa.

f   Lucy, **who** / **which** scored all five goals in the game on Saturday, hurt her knee in the game this afternoon.

2 Write sentences using *who* or *which*.

a   Miss Lawson studied at Colombia University. <u>Extra information:</u> She is my art teacher.
    <u>Miss Lawson, who is my art teacher, studied at Colombia University.</u>

b   I got an A in Spanish. <u>Extra information:</u> It's my favorite subject.

c   My sister works as a TV host of a morning news show. <u>Extra information:</u> She lives in Boston.

d   The painter Rembrandt is often called an "Old Master." <u>Extra information:</u> He was born in the Netherlands in the 16th century.

e   Last weekend, we saw the new superhero film. <u>Extra information:</u> I didn't like it.

Writing: A Biography

1 READ Read the biography. Why didn't George Eliot use her own name for her books?

A Biography of George Eliot

Mary Ann Evans, who is better known as George Eliot, was one of the great writers of the 19th century. She helped develop the art of the novel and remains an important cultural figure.

George Eliot was born Mary Ann Evans in England in 1819. After she finished school, she continued to educate herself in her spare time. For several years, she worked in London as a translator, a writer of essays, and a book reviewer.

When she was in her thirties, Mary Ann Evans began to write stories, which she published under the pen name George Eliot. She did this because women were not taken seriously as artists or writers. The public learned of George Eliot's true identity after her second book, *Adam Bede*, which was published in 1859, made her famous. By the 1870s, she was one of the most famous novelists in the world. Even Queen Victoria read her books!

George Eliot's most well-known novels are *The Mill on the Floss* and *Middlemarch*. My favorite, however, is *Silas Marner*, which is the story of a kind man who adopts a little girl named Eppie.

2 EXPLORE Match the excerpts from the biography to the phrases.

1 an introduction to the person _____
2 key dates in the person's life _____
3 an interesting detail about the person's life _____
4 an opinion about the person and their work _____

a By the 1870s, she was one of the most famous novelists in the world.
b For several years, she worked in London as a translator, a writer of essays, and a book reviewer.
c Mary Ann Evans, who is better known as George Eliot, was one of the great writers of the 19th century.
d My favorite, however, is *Silas Marner*, which is the story of a kind man who adopts a little girl named Eppie.

3 **PLAN** Think of a famous person from the past to write about. This person could be a king or a queen, an artist, a writer, a musician, an athlete, or anyone else you would like to write about. Research some information about the person. Complete the graphic organizer.

Introduction

_____
_____

Key Dates

_____
_____

A Biography Of

_____

Interesting Details About Their Life

_____
_____

My Opinion About Their Life and Work

_____
_____

4 **WRITE** Write your biography. Use your notes from Activity 3.

_____
_____
_____
_____
_____
_____

CHECK

Did you …
- include an introduction to the person? ☐
- include key dates in the person's life? ☐
- include an interesting detail about the person's life? ☐
- include an opinion about the person and their work? ☐
- include a non-defining relative clause? ☐

Practice Your Exam Skills

Complete the email. Fill in each blank with one word.

FROM: Dylan
TO: Sofia

Hi Sofia,

I'm glad 1 ____you____. had a good summer. We had 2 _____ great time in England! We went to the Jurassic Coast. Do you know it? You can search there for fossils—the remains of plants 3 _____ animals from millions of years ago! Fossils 4 _____ first found there in the early 19th century.

We searched on Charmouth beach, 5 _____ was near our hotel. I picked something up and said, "This 6 _____ be a part of a dinosaur. It kind of looks like a tooth." Dad replied, "We can't be sure, Dylan, but anything is possible here." We didn't actually find any fossils, but I 7 _____ mind. We're going back next summer!

Let's meet up soon.

Dylan

SEND

9 Why does biodiversity matter?

Grammar: The Second Conditional

If A Poem by Chloe Galt

1 If I had the opportunity, I would change the world I love,
I would make it right for creatures from below to up above,
I would save the humpback whales that swim so far in the ocean deep
and the dark turtle doves that often wake me from my sleep.

5 If I could make decisions, I would keep the forests green,
I would ban the use of plastics and would make the rivers clean.
If I could, I'd stop the pipes that pump the waste into the seas,
and I'd ask my friends to join me in the planting of new trees.

9 You see we must think about the world in every way
and how we need to change the things we do and what we say.
The Earth's the only home we have, remember that today,
and its future depends on how we work and play.

13 If there were no bees, there wouldn't be so much for us to eat.
If there were no trees, the air we need to breathe would not be sweet.
If we changed our ways, we wouldn't have to worry about things.
We'd enjoy our world, and life itself, and all the joy it brings.

1) Read the poem. What does Chloe say about the Earth in line 11?

2) Complete the sentences with verbs. Are these verbs past or present tense? Is Chloe's poem about the past or about the present and future?

a   If I _____ the opportunity, I would change the world I love.
b   If I _____ make decisions, I would keep the forests green.
c   If there _____ no bees, there wouldn't be so much for us to eat.
d   If there _____ no trees, the air we need to breathe would not be sweet.

83

Grammar: The Second Conditional

We use the second conditional to describe situations in the present or future that are hypothetical, unlikely, or impossible. We use the following form: *if* + verb in the past simple in one part of the sentence + *would/wouldn't* + base verb in the other part.

We use a comma when *if* is used in the first part of the sentence but not when *if* is used in the second part of the sentence.

If we **used** less plastic, the ocean **would be** cleaner.

We **wouldn't have** so much pollution **if** we **didn't burn** so many fossil fuels.

If I **was** an animal, I **would be** a bird. I would love to fly around the world!

Remember: *would* can be abbreviated as *'d*.

3. Circle the correct verb to make second conditional sentences.

a If we **grow / (grew)** our own vegetables, we wouldn't need to go to supermarkets all the time.

b I would **watch / watched** a movie tonight if we didn't have an English test tomorrow.

c If I **meet / met** an American movie star, I would ask them questions about Hollywood.

d If I **can / could** travel in time, I would go back to the time of the dinosaurs.

e If I went to the International Space Station, I would **take / took** photographs of the Earth.

f It would be great if we **have / had** a bigger house.

4. Complete the sentences with the verbs in parentheses and your own ideas.

a If I had more time, _I would learn to play the piano._ (learn)

b If I could live in any country, _____ (live)

c If I had a lot of money, _____ (buy)

d If I went to New York, _____ (visit)

e If I could be any animal, _____ (be)

f If I could go back in time, _____ (go)

5) **Complete the sentences. Use the verbs in the box in the correct form.**

   a If we ___didn't pollute___ the rivers, the fish ___would have___ cleaner water.

   b If we _____ down the forests, millions of species _____ their habitat.

   c If we _____ fossil fuels, we _____ the level of carbon dioxide in the atmosphere.

   d If we _____ the planet better, fewer animals _____ extinct.

   e If we _____ the oceans, we _____ the coral reefs from disappearing.

   > not lose   reduce   clean
   > take care of   ~~have~~   not cut
   > become   ~~not pollute~~
   > not burn   stop

6) **Read the situation. Write a second conditional sentence.**

   a I don't have enough money. I can't buy a computer.
   If I had enough money, I would buy a computer.

   b I have a cell phone. I send so many text messages.
   _____

   c I don't run quickly. I don't win races at school.
   _____

   d I have lots of homework to do. I won't go to the party.
   _____

   e I don't live in the countryside. I don't breathe fresh air.
   _____

7) **Answer the questions with your own ideas. Use the second conditional.**

   a What would happen if our cities became more polluted?
   _____

   b What would happen if we didn't have any rain?
   _____

Grammar: Embedded Questions

A Question of Politeness

Mr. Curry thought the students in his new English class were very intelligent. They worked very hard. However, there was one thing they didn't always do so well: ask questions politely. These were the kinds of questions they produced:

"What is the test about?"
"When is the game?"
"Are you from Ireland?"

Of course, when we're talking to our close friends or members of our family, such direct questions are fine. However, in school, we need a different kind of question. This is why Mr. Curry taught his students to say:

"Can you tell me what the test is about?"
"Do you know when the game is?"
"I wonder if you're from Ireland."

Before long, the students knew how to politely ask Mr. Curry a question. Today, after a very interesting science class with Miss Walters, the students asked him about biodiversity and the future of the planet:

"Can you tell me what global warming is?"
"Do you know what carbon dioxide is?"
"I wonder why animals become extinct."

1. Read the story. What did Mr. Curry teach his class?

2. Complete the questions from the story.

   a What **is the test** about? _____ what the test is about?

   b When **is the game**? _____ when the game is?

   c **Are you** from Ireland? _____ if you're from Ireland.

3. Look at the questions in Activity 2. How do the highlighted words in each first question change in the second question?

_____

Grammar: Embedded Questions

An embedded question is a question we put inside another question or a statement.
  Can you tell me what I should do?
  Do you know where Ramin lives?
  I wonder what time the match is.

An embedded question is more polite than a direct question. In addition, its word order is different. Compare:

Direct Question	Embedded Question
What time is it?	Can you tell me what time it is?
Where does Sasha live?	Do you know where Sasha lives?

Remember: After an embedded question that begins *Can you tell me* … or *Do you know* … , we use a question mark. After *I wonder* … , we use a period.

4 Read the embedded questions. Write the direct questions.

a Can you tell me when the show starts?
  When does the show start?

b Do you know what day the party is?
  _____

c Do you know where Sam's house is?
  _____

d I wonder how dolphins communicate.
  _____

e I wonder what your favorite movie is.
  _____

5 Complete the embedded questions with *Can you*, *Do you*, or *I wonder*.

a ____*Do you*____ know what time the movie starts?

b _____ who is going to the party.

c _____ tell me where the park is?

d _____ what "ecosystem" means.

e _____ tell me what Lou is doing?

f _____ know where my bag is?

6 Complete the embedded questions.

a When does chess club meet? Can you tell me when chess club meets?
b Where does Mirko live? I wonder _____
c Where is the classroom? Do you know _____
d Are you free on Saturday afternoon? I wonder _____
e What is the biggest shark? Do you know _____

7 Write three embedded questions for each of the direct questions.

a When does the train leave?

Can you tell me when the train leaves?

Do you know when the train leaves?

I wonder when the train leaves.

b What time is the chemistry test?

_____
_____
_____

c What kind of music does she like?

_____
_____
_____

d How long is the flight to Los Angeles?

_____
_____
_____

8 Read the text. Decide what questions you want to ask. Then, write polite questions using *Do you know … ? Can you tell me … ?* and *I wonder … .*

You are on vacation in Paris with your family. You've never been there before, and you're a bit lost! You'd like to visit famous places like the Louvre Museum, the Arc de Triomphe, the Pantheon (where the great scientist Marie Curie is buried), and the Pont Neuf (the oldest standing bridge in the city). But you don't know where they are! You stop a woman on the street. You'd like to know if she knows where places are and how to get to them. You'd also like her to tell you about a good restaurant where you can have some lunch.

_____
_____
_____
_____

Improve Your Writing

Although

Although is a connecting word like *and*, *because*, *however*, and many others. *Although* means "despite the fact that" or "but." *Although* is used at the beginning or in the middle of a sentence and is followed by a subject and a verb.

Although it was cold, we went swimming in the outdoor pool.
(Despite the fact that it was cold, we went swimming in the outdoor pool.)
We're going the movies tonight, although I don't know when.
(We're going to the movies tonight, but I don't know when.)

1 Complete the sentences with *although* and a sentence from the box.

> I didn't know anyone
> she works 80 hours a week
> I found biology difficult at first
> she's only been playing for six months
> ~~we know a lot about plant and animal life on Earth~~

a *Although we know a lot about plant and animal life on Earth*, there are many species for human beings to discover.

b _____ at my new school, everyone was friendly and welcomed me.

c _____, it's become my favorite subject.

d My sister plays the piano really well, _____.

e My mom enjoys being a doctor, _____.

2 Rewrite the sentences. Use *although*.

a Joe enjoyed the party. He was tired.
   Joe enjoyed the party, although he was tired.   *Although Joe was tired, he enjoyed the party.*

b Callum passed the exam. He didn't study hard.
   _____   _____

c Lea played in the soccer game. She was injured.
   _____   _____

d We went out. It was raining.
   _____   _____

Writing: A Flyer

 **READ** Read the flyer. Why should we avoid using products containing palm oil?

SAVE THE SUMATRAN ORANGUTAN!

Sumatran orangutans live in the tropical rainforest in the north of the Indonesian island of Sumatra. They spend most of their time in the trees. Although male orangutans are usually alone, female orangutans move around with their young.

Unfortunately, the Sumatran orangutan is one of the world's most endangered animals. In the past, there were orangutans all over the island of Sumatra, but now they are found only in the north. There are nine groups, with only three having more than 1,000 orangutans.

Why is this animal endangered? The orangutans' rainforest habitat is being destroyed in order to plant palm oil trees. The fruit of these trees produce an oil that is sold around the world. In addition, orangutans are captured and kept in people's homes, even though this activity has been illegal in Indonesia since 1931.

What can we do?

- Donate money to a wildlife organization.
- Don't use products that contain palm oil.
- Become a volunteer and help restore the Sumatran rainforest.

If we all did something, we could help save this beautiful animal. Don't waste any more time—join our campaign and start doing something now!

 **EXPLORE** Read the three sentences from the flyer. Then, answer the questions.

1. The orangutans' rainforest habitat is being destroyed in order to plant palm oil trees.
2. Donate money to a wildlife organization.
3. Don't waste any more time—join our campaign and start doing something now!

a Which sentence gives the reader practical advice? _____
b Which sentence encourages the reader to take action? _____
c Which sentence describes why the animal is endangered? _____

3 PLAN You are going to write a flyer about the African elephant. Research information about the animal and make notes.

1 Which African countries does it live in? (Include the names of countries, and tell which parts of the countries.)

2 How does it live? (Where does it spend its time? What does it eat?)

3 Why is it endangered? (Give at least two reasons.)

4 What can we do? (Offer at least two practical ideas.)

4 WRITE Write your flyer. Use your notes from Activity 3 to help you.

CHECK

Did you …
- describe why the animal is endangered? ☐
- encourage the reader to take action? ☐
- give the reader practical advice? ☐
- include *although*? ☐

Practice Your Exam Skills

Read the article about sharks. Choose the best word (A, B, or C) for each space.

Sharks

Part of a **1** ___family___ of animals that evolved more than 400 million years ago, sharks are marine fish. They have a large dorsal fin, **2** _____ skin is covered in tooth-like scales, and they have a skeleton made from cartilage, similar to the material human ears and noses are made of. Most sharks are predatory. They are the top of the food chain and **3** _____ on small fish. **4** _____, some of the biggest sharks eat only plankton, the small organisms that float in seawater.

There are over five hundred species of sharks. The biggest is the whale shark, and the most well-known is the great white. Sadly, many sharks are **5** _____ due to overfishing and illegal hunting. The balance of the ocean's ecosystem **6** _____ on these animals, which is why they need to be protected.

1	A relation	B family	C parents
2	A their	B its	C her
3	A eat	B feed	C have
4	A In addition	B Therefore	C However
5	A wild	B dangerous	C endangered
6	A depends	B decides	C affects

Review: Units 1–3

Read the text. Choose the right words and write them in the blanks.

September 25

Dear friends and neighbors,

Come to our fundraising event for the victims of Hurricane Robert. The event **1** __will__ take place on October 10 at Grange Road School, at 2 p.m.

Hurricane Robert happened six months **2** _____, but people are still suffering the consequences. **3** _____ people on the island of Kathik had to leave their homes, and **4** _____ were unable to return because their homes were destroyed.

The buildings on the island are not **5** _____ to withstand natural disasters. In addition, news of the hurricane didn't reach the island until it was **6** _____ late. There wasn't **7** _____ time to protect the island.

At the fundraising event, we will be having games and a concert. We **8** _____ raise **9** _____ money to really make a difference in people's lives.

Anyone who would like to volunteer to set up the event, please contact Mrs. Thompson. All volunteers will be given a job to do; you can never have too **10** _____ helpers!

Thank you,

The students of Grange Road School

1	is	going to	will
2	ago	past	before
3	No	Most	A few
4	some	no	everyone
5	design	designed	designing
6	too	enough	too much
7	many	too	enough
8	going to	might	won't
9	too much	enough	not enough
10	much	many	enough

Review: Units 4–6

Read the text. Choose the right words and write them in the blanks.

How Do Movies Get Made?

I am a film student. I've **1** _been_ studying cinema for three years now, and I've been **2** _____ my own short movies **3** _____ I was 12. People think that movies get made easily, but I've learned that isn't the case. In fact, it's very difficult to get a movie made.

First of all, the movie is **4** _____ . But **5** _____ writes the movie? Someone who writes movies or TV programs is called a screenwriter. When the writing stage is complete, people read the screenplay and decide if they want to finance the movie.

Next, preparations are made to shoot the movie. This involves hiring actors, directors, and cameramen. This sounds exciting, **6** _____ it isn't straightforward and often involves negotiation. In my last short movie, the actors asked if they **7** _____ get paid more. They said that they **8** _____ working too hard.

When everything is ready, the shooting begins. (The shooting for my next short movie **9** _____ next week.) The final stage is known as post-production. This is when the movie is edited and the special effects are added.

The whole process of making a movie is incredibly expensive. I wish I **10** _____ more money!

1	have	was	been
2	made	make	making
3	for	since	before
4	written	write	all
5	who	when	what
6	and	but	if
7	can	can't	could
8	are	was	were
9	going to start	starting	starts
10	had	have	have had

Review: Units 7-9

Read the text. Choose the right words and write them in the blanks.

Name: Dan Marcus

Report Topic: Nature Reserve

Last week, my class **1** __went__ to the Lake View Nature Reserve in Hailsford. It was an amazing trip.

The nature reserve is made up of more than 70 square kilometers of grassland and water. It **2** _____ established in 1875 and is home to thousands of species of plants and animals. The guide **3** _____ us that animals like falcons, owls, deer, raccoons, and snakes live here.

These species of plants and animals **4** _____ protected in the nature reserve. They cannot be harmed by pollution or hunting. If I could change the world, I **5** _____ all animals and plants.

We saw a type of bird that is on the protected species list. Next year, you will **6** _____ see eagles. They are going to be introduced to the reserve. We saw a lot of deer. I love deer. If people didn't hunt them so much, there **7** _____ be more of them. There was a small group of them, which ran away when they saw us. They **8** _____ be afraid of small children!

It was amazing to be in the middle of nature, away from the noisy city! The scenery is beautiful. I **9** _____ if you've ever seen such beautiful scenery. I **10** _____ come and visit the reserve if I were you!

1	been	went	visit
2	was	is	were
3	told	said	tell
4	is	was	are
5	protect	protected	would protect
6	can	be able to	could
7	will	can	would
8	are	will	must
9	think	curious	wonder
10	would	should	could

95

Thanks and Acknowledgments

The authors and publishers acknowledge the following sources of copyright material and are grateful for the permissions granted. While every effort has been made, it has not always been possible to identify the sources of all the material used or to trace all copyright holders. If any omissions are brought to our notice, we will be happy to include the appropriate acknowledgments on reprinting and in the next update to the digital edition, as applicable.

Photography

All the photographs are sourced from Getty Images.

Cover photography by Westend6I - Gerald Nowak/Brand X Pictures/Getty Images; abadonian/iStock/Getty Images; vlad6I/iStock/Getty Images; Marcoriveroph/iStock/Getty Images; wildestanimal/Moment/Getty Images.

Illustration

Collaborate Agency.

Cover illustrations by Monica Armino (Advocate).

Typesetting

Blooberry Design and QBS Learning.